WILD
swimming
ITALY

Discover the most beautiful
rivers, lakes, waterfalls
and hot springs of Italy

Michele Tameni

For my mother, who supported me in every adventure

WILD
swimming
ITALY

Contents

Swims by region

Wild Swimming Italy begins its journey in the north east, in the foothills of the Alps, with the emerald streams and pools of the Friulian Dolomites and the bright colours of the Trentino lakes. We cross to the Great Lakes of Lombardia, including the huge and famous lakes of Como and Garda, their shores loved by tourists rights back to Roman times. Here we can point you to many hidden beaches, and some less-discovered lakes too, but you will also find gorges, waterfalls and breathtaking valley views.

The Piedmont region in Italy's north west harbours wild mountain pools, with water temperatures warming as you head towards down to the valleys and the lowlands facing the Ligurian sea. Crossing over the border into the idyllic Tuscan hills you can relax in thermal pools surrounded by dark forest. Discover the gentle rivers of Tuscany too, and magical pools like those at Candalla, set among ruined mills and lush forests.

Cross the Apennines - the central mountain spine of Italy - to Emilia Romagna in the east, where the peculiar rock type and the action of water have created fantastic places like Grotta Urlante and Zerbale, the queen of all pools.

Southbound, landscapes vary quickly. There are volcanic lakes in the Marche region and in Lazio, huge rocky 'marmitte' carved from the rivers, and great waterfalls pools such as Lake Pellicone. Visit the verdant valley of the Castellano river, Lake Fiastra and the unforgettable Marmore waterfall.

In Abruzzo the Apennines show their most dramatic nature in a land of dizzying gorges and emerald rock pools, but once in Campania, in the deep south, the land becomes drier. So head for the wild heartland of the little-known Cilento National Park. Here find the blue sources of Sammaro and Capelli di Venere waterfall. Finally to the islands of Sicily and Sardinia, better known for their coast, head for the interior to seek out spectacular basalt gorges, remote waterfalls and valleys immersed in a flowers and fragrant scrub.

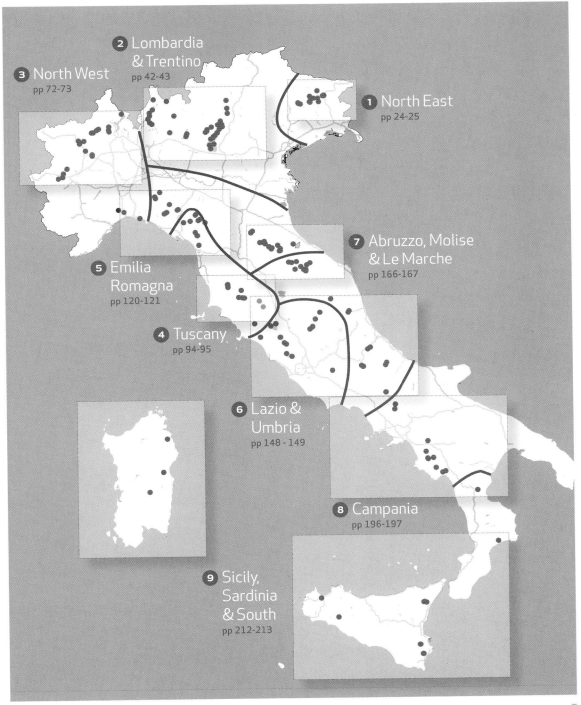

2 Lombardia
& Trentino
pp 42-43

3 North West
pp 72-73

1 North East
pp 24-25

7 Abruzzo, Molise
& Le Marche
pp 166-167

5 Emilia
Romagna
pp 120-121

4 Tuscany
pp 94-95

6 Lazio &
Umbria
pp 148 - 149

8 Campania
pp 196-197

9 Sicily,
Sardinia
& South
pp 212-213

Introduction

The air was already warm; a golden haze rose from the waterfall. The morning light played on the green leaves of the forest and sunbeams danced through the jade pool. I took a deep breath, two more steps, then leapt into the oasis.

Diving deep down to touch the pebbles on the river floor, I rose ecstatic in a riot of bubbles. It was the beginning of a new day on a journey to find Italy's most beautiful natural swimming pools.

This book is an invitation to wild swimming in Italy. Dive into our hidden waters and discover parts of the landscape that few people ever find. Enjoy the age-old pursuits of having fun by the river, or enjoying a sunset swim from a lake shore.

Away from the famous coastline of the peninsula, and the great cities of art, there is a wild and varied Italy that hides mysterious gorges and natural springs; river pools, lakes and magnificent waterfalls to match any in the world. Many places are close to the major tourist spots, so make a perfect interlude from the heat of the city. Most places are suitable for all - young and old - while some are reserved only for the adventurous.

Wild Swimming Italy retraces our journey over three summers, pawing over maps, travelling from village to village asking local people to reveal the secret places, walking and hiking to find and test the most beautiful places to swim.

So there is no need to travel to far-flung parts of the globe to find paradise this summer. Magical corners of the forest await, where you can commune with nature, detox from urban stresses, or simply find reprieve from the summer heat, even if it's just for an afternoon.

Wild swimming phrases and glossary

Can you recommend a good river or lake swimming spot near here? *C'è un bel posto vicino per fare un bagno in un lago o in un fiume?*

Is it deep enough for diving? *È abbastanza profondo per tuffarsi?*

Is the pool large enough to swim? *La pozza/laghetto e' abbastanza grande per nuotare?*

Is the water clean enough for swimming? *L'acqua e' abbastanza pulita per fare il bagno?*

Is it nice for children? *E' adeguata per i bambini?*

Where is the nicest section (of the lake / river) for swimming? *Dov'e' la parte migliore (del lago/fiume) per nuotare/fare un bagno?*

Is swimming allowed here / there? *E' permesso fare il bagno qui/la?*

Swimming in a natural setting/ swimming outdoors - *Nuotare in un ambiente naturale/ Nuotare nella natura*

Lago – *lake*

Valle – *valley*

Gole - *gorges*

Grotta - *cave*

Terme - *hot spring / spa*

Spiaggia / lido – *beach*

Cascata / salto - *waterfall*

Fiume / torrente / fosso –*river or stream*

Riva del fiume – *river bank*

Sponda – *shore*

Ansa / mulino - *mill*

Sbarramento / diga - *weir / dam*

Vasca di accumulo - *reservoir (man made)*

Nuotare - *to swim*

Tuffarsi - *to dive/jump*

Acqua dolce - *fresh water*

Nuoto selvaggio - *wild swimming*

Bagno nel fiume - *river swimming*

Luogo di balneazione - *swimming place*

Piscina / pozza / laghetto / gorga / goja – *natural pool*

Sorgente/Risorgenza - *spring where water or a river emerges from underground*

Piscina/Vasca/Bacina - *large pool or basin of water*

Marmitta - *deeply eroded 'pot' or tub in rock (filled with water)*

Swimming prohibited - *Divieto di balneazione*

Upstream / Downstream – *a monte / a valle*

Left bank / right bank - *riva sinistra/ riva destra*

North / east / south / west – *nord / est / sud / ovest*

Northern / eastern / southern / western - *settentrionale / orientale / meridionale / occidentale*

Ten ways to be wild and safe

1. Downstream of hydroelectric dams, pay attention to changes in water level.

2. Do not explore narrow gorges if rainstorms are expected upstream.

3. Don't swim in canals, urban rivers or stagnant ponds. Cover cuts and wounds with waterproof plasters if you are unsure of the water quality.

4. Never swim in swollen rivers and beware of water quality in dry periods.

5. Do not swim alone and keep a constant check on weak swimmers.

6. Never jump into water unless you have thoroughly checked it for depth.

7. Make sure you know how to get out before entering the water.

8. Do not get cold. Do warm-up exercises before a swim and put on warm clothes straight after. A wetsuit is useful in colder rivers.

9. Wear appropriate footwear, both in and out the water.

10. Wear sunscreen. While swimming, it's easy to forget how strong the sun can be.

Turn to pages 252-253 for more information on safety and access.

The hot Italian summers are the perfect time to take a dip in the pools and waterfalls of our countryside. It's a perfect way to complement a walk or day out, and a swimming spot always makes a good destination for a picnic lunch.

Fortunately the mild climate of the South allows you to enjoy wild swimming in the spring and well into the autumn too. The thermal pools, with temperatures reaching well over 50C are ideal destinations for winter evenings.

What to bring - You do not need much: a swimming costume, a pair of comfortable shoes and a towel will suffice in most cases. Aqua shoes or sandals are excellent for scrambling around on the rocks and essential if you are planning to explore gorges or walk for long distances along a river bed. Hiking boots are recommended for sites that require longer walks and a normal sleeveless wetsuit can help children stay warm when swimming in colder mountain streams. Do not forget sunscreen, especially in the mountains where the cool air can easily deceive, and insect repellent for evenings in the woods.

Unexpected dips - If you find a beautiful and inviting natural swimming pool during a walk, don't be shy. Use your underwear as a swimming costume or skinny-dip if the place is secluded. Afterwards wipe most of the water off with your hands and simply dry off in the sun, or sacrifice one item of your clothing to act as your towel. It's a good idea to always carry a small cotton sarong, or microfiber towel.

Wild camping - This is illegal in Italy and fires during dry periods can be very dangerous. If you decide to camp be discreet and invisible. Leave no trace. Be careful if camping close to the bank of a river or stream, as rain or storms upstream may create sudden flooding and wash you away.

FINDING YOUR WAY

You can reach the locations using the overview road maps and the detailed location maps in the annex. Ideally you will also have a road atlas. Use these in combination with the directions and the latitude/longitude co-ordinates. The co-ordinates can be entered into any mobile or computer mapping app or website (e.g. Google maps) to bring up online maps and satellite imagery. Make sure to print these out - or save a screen shot - before you leave home, in case there is limited signal. You can also enter the co-ordinates into a GPS device or app. Trailzilla and Viewranger apps help turn your phone into a mobile satnav.

Walk-in times and walk difficulty are also given and symbols indicate the presence of campsites, restaurants and rentals of canoes and paddle boats, with phone numbers.

To find your own location - If you have detailed maps available - the best for Italy are the Kompass maps at scales of 1:25,000 or 1:50,000 scale - look for the tight bends of rivers, where beaches and deep sections can form - or areas below dams and weirs.

Almost all lakes are accessible, but in artificial lakes stay away from the dams. Rivers suitable for canoeing are often deep enough for swimming, and other interesting locations can be found in canyoning books. Canyon entry and exit points are often beautiful and interesting and relatively easy to reach .

Best for Hot Springs

Wild and natural - hot mineral waters in which to soak and cleanse while gazing up at the forest or stars

Best for Blue Pools

The most azure, emerald, jade or aquamarine waters you'll find this side of the Seychelles

Best for Waterfalls

Magically situated under waterfalls, big and small

Best for Campsites

Our favourite river and lakeside campsites - wake up with a swim!

Best for History & Ruins

Swim beneath great castles and enjoy the history of Italy from the water

Best for Jumping

Deep pools with great leaps. Take care!

Best for Waterside Food

Close to a taverna or recommended place to eat

17	Bogliaco	98A	Spiaggia Berlina
18	Le Fontanelle, Gargnano	104B	Bolsena
20	Limone sul Garda	131	Lago di Scanno
73	Candalla	84B	Mulino della
97	Lido del Groppo		sega e Ca' Ridolla

Best for Skinny Dipping

Swim as nature intended in remote and beautiful locations

7	Pozze Smeraldine	61	Cascata del serpente
13	Campone	76B	Lago Paduli
15	Rocca di Manerba	80	La Para
57	Goja del Pis	147B	Cavagrande del Cassibile

Best for Kids & Families

Mainly shallow with shelving beaches. Perfect for family fun

2	Torrente Cellina	77B	La Morra
9	Lago di Cavazzo	79	Fiume Marecchia
20	Limone sul Garda	93	Ansa dei Graniti
25	Lago di Ledro	98A	Spiaggia Berlina
27	Lago di Molveno	108	Lago di Martignano
44C	Spiaggia Boschina	114	Le Piscine dell'Auro
68	Quarciglione, Solaia	127	Villa Santa Maria
69	Fiume Merse	139	Fiume Carole, Castelcivita
74	Lago di Gramolazzo	142	Cascata Capelli di Venere

Best for Canoeing & Boats

Hire a canoe, pedalo or punt, and find your own secret swim

Best for Wild Camping

Wonderful and wild locations for sleeping out by the water - remember no fires and always be discrete

Best for Canyons

Dramatic rock shapes, formations and gorges that will leave you awe-struck

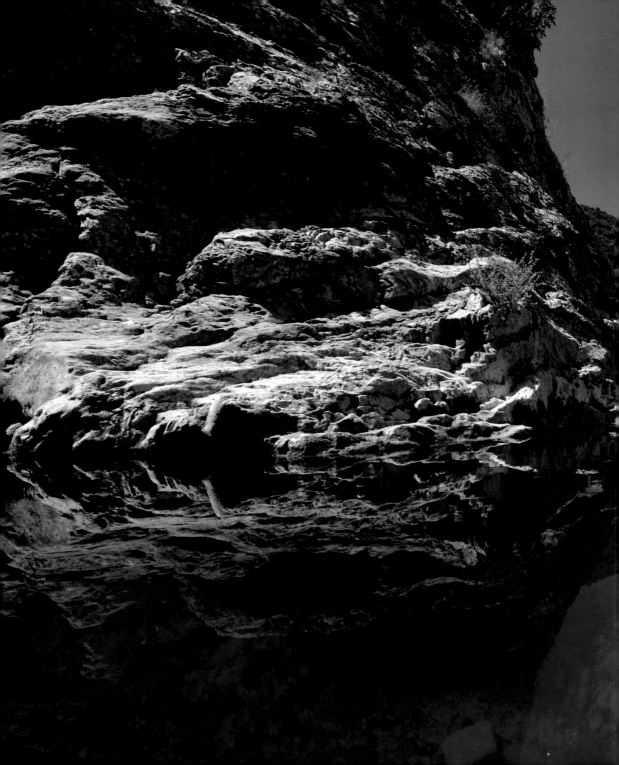

Torrente Palar, upper pools where the valley narrows

North East

Among the rugged Dolomites of Friuli, emerald-coloured rivers flow into wild valleys, and cross wonderfully shaped canyons, between white rocks and foaming waterfalls.

Highlights North East

Our favourites include:

8 Cascata Plera - a blue pool beneath a waterfall that flows into a funnel of rock; beautiful forest and ancient fortifications

7 Pozze Smeraldine -amazing emerald colour water, isolated and secluded in a magnificent natural setting

10 Torrente Palar- a popular creek with many pools, narrowing as you go upstream

12 Cerdevol - spectacular white canyon with clear aquamarine pools

SS52
PARCO NATURALE DOLOMITI FRIULANE
Longarone
SP20
Cimolais
Villanova
SS51
Torrente Cellina
1
2
3
Lago di Barcis
Maniago
A27
SP19
Lago di Santa Croce

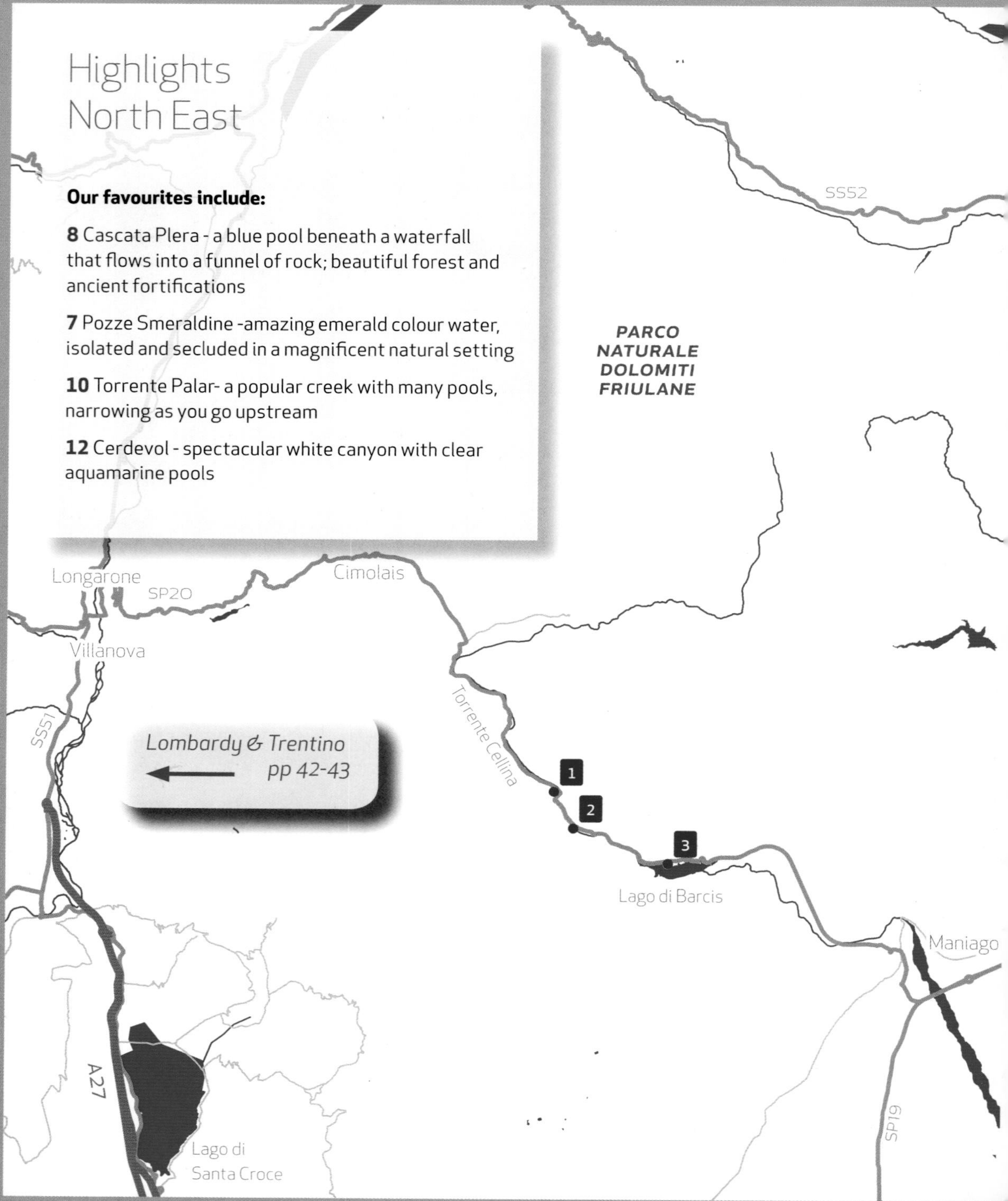

Lombardy & Trentino pp 42-43

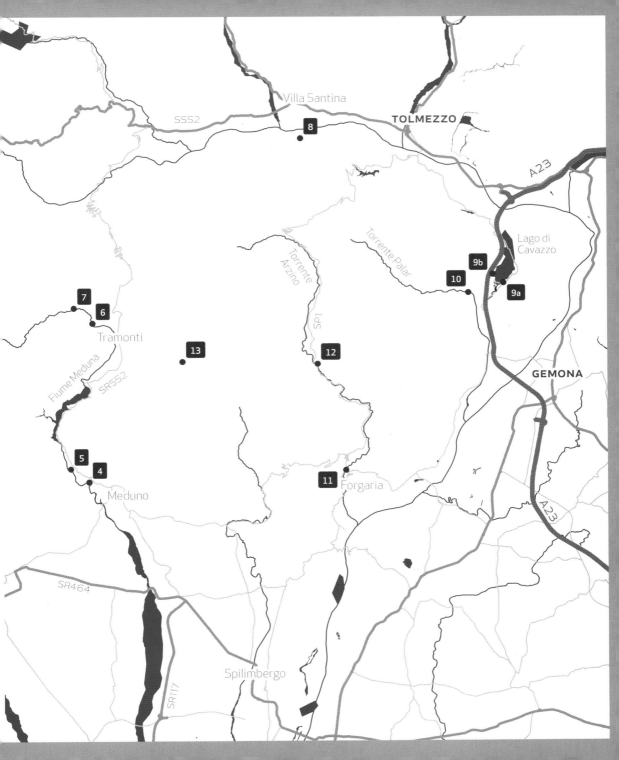

2 Torrente Cellina

3

The landscape in the North East Italian alpine zone has a difficult terrain, consisting of narrow valleys of poor soils often subject to landslides, crossed by flowing rivers and streams. Such features do not make life easy for those who decide to live there, but they do make for some breathtaking views to those hikers who venture there today.

The toughness of the landscape is easily visible as you leave the Veneto region, at the village of Longarone, and head east up on the S251 past the site of the Vajont Dam disaster. The narrow, deep and somewhat gloomy gorge overlooked by the dam is intimidating, and reminds us of the respect we owe to nature. One night in 1963, over 500 million tonnes of rock slid into the reservoir, creating a giant wave that killed over 2,000 people sleeping in the valley below.

▶

Valcellina, Dolomiti Friulane Natural Park

1 TORRENTE PROVAGNA

You can reach the small gorge of this stream from the broad gravel bed of the Cellina river. The first part is easy going and accessible to all. Further up the river the path gets more complicated but the unspoilt and wild setting of the narrow valley and the jade green pools justify the effort. There are a couple of fascinating pools at the far end (about 3km).

➜ Driving along the A27 northbound, take the SS51 towards Cortina. Entering Longarone, turn R to take the SR251 towards Erto/Vajont Dam. Continue for another 28km, passing the impressive dam and the towns of Erto and Cimolais. Cross the bridge over the River Cellina, another bridge over a stream feeding into the river, and stop on the L just before the next bridge (Mezzo Canale). Park your car and follow the river until you see the entrance to the narrow valley of Provagna on your R. The first pools are close and easy but it will take up to two hours to visit the final pools.

3 mins easy, 46.2124, 12.5086

2 TORRENTE CELLINA

Along its course, the Cellina river flows over a broad gravel bed, passing through beautiful steep valleys, creating a magnificent backdrop with its unusual colour. A few miles before the village of Barcis, the river creates several ponds and pools – the water is clear and cold and it's easy to find a spot where you can be completely on your own.

➜ Continue for 1.5km along the SR251 from Torrente Provagna (73km marker) and park in a narrow road on the R. Look out for a wooden gate and a bulletin board with the sign 'Foresta del Prescudin'. Look on the L for a small trail that goes down to the river. Further up the course, the pools become much deeper.

3 mins easy, 46.2008, 12.5171

3 LAGO DI BARCIS

This picturesque turquoise lake is surrounded by mountains. In the village of Barcis there is a small public beach with lovely grassy banks. A visit to the beautiful Cellina gorge, reachable from a pedestrian road on the eastern side of the lake, is a must.

➜ From the Cellina river just continue on the SR251 and you will get to Barcis. Park in the car park just outside the village, and walk along the cycling/pedestrian route that starts on the L, before the parking area. Coming from Maniago, take the SR251 NW-bound and in 16km you will come to Barcis. The car park is at the beginning of the village and is linked by the same cycling/pedestrian route mentioned above.

1 min easy, 46.1898, 12.5588

Fiume Meduna

4

6

Head over the pass, into the Dolomiti Friulane Natural Park and down into the Cellina valley, where you will find many wild, unspoilts pools and gorges on the way to the small village of Barcis. The Torrente Provagna 1 runs through a small gorge off the Cellina river. Make time to hike all the way into its upper reaches. Next along the SR251 is the beautiful Forra del Cellina: an amazing gorge and wild canyon with steep cliffs that plunge into the clear waters of the creek, with good swimming just upstream 2. Finally, a little way on, is Lago di Barcis 3, a turquoise, glass-like lake with a wide variety of watersports.

Head through Maniago, a village in the province of Pordenone famous since medieval times for its cutlery manufacture, towards the Meduna valley. Travel towards the village of Meduno, where you will find a couple of shingle beaches by spectacular green river pools 4. This is a secluded corner to cool down, surrounded by nature.

Further along the SR552 the Lago dei Tramonti (Sunset Lake) is interesting to visit because, hidden beneath the waters, you will find the ruins of the old houses of the village of Flors, which emerge like a mirage in the dry season. Stay overnight in Tramonti di Sotto, at a campsite in the woods with river access, and then travel up to Tramonti di Sopra, where you will find ▶

4 Fiume Meduno

The Meduna Valley and Tramonti

4 FIUME MEDUNA

Two beautiful river pools: one under a bridge (from which you can dive), the other shaped around a strange rock like a pyramid. The gravel beach is large, and small trees and bushes provide shelter from the sun.

➜ From Maniago take the SP2 NE as far as Meduno and turn L on to the SR552, signposted Tramonti. After 800m take the turn for Preplans and go as far as the bridge. Park your car and go down to the river from the road on the L after the bridge. The first large and deep pool is under the bridge - ford the river and follow it upstream to find the second pool.

3 mins easy, 46.2191, 12.7722

5 NAVARONS

Nestled in the woods but close to town, this is a lovely place. A large green lake with small scattered beaches and shrubs, where the water flows slowly and quietly.

➜ Continue a little further along the SR552 in the direction of Tramonti. Pass the village of Pitagora and turn L for Navarons. After 200m park at the first bend to the R, and continue walking along to the next bend (to the L). There is a wall at the bend and a path above and into the woods on the R. Go into the woods and down to the river, until you get to the beach.

5 mins easy, 46.2262, 12.7593

6 TRAMONTI DI SOPRA

A large picnic area right on the bank of the river, dotted with small fir trees. A couple of small lakes are located not far away, but it is worth going up the river 500m to where the bed narrows and passes between some very scenic rocks.

➜ Continue 4km N along the SR552 to Tramonti di Sotto. Pass the bridge over the River Viellia, carry on to the wide turning on the L and then, after the shrine, turn L towards the picnic area. Turn L again and continue for about 1.5km. Between Tramonti di Sopra and Tramonti di Sotto, in Sottoriva, there is an attractive camping site in the woods, with access to the river: ▲ Campeggia Valtramontina

(Tel 0427 869004). The people are very friendly at this campsite - we fully recommend it.

1 min easy, 46.3018, 12.7753

7 POZZE SMERALDINE

The colour of these beautiful, natural pools justifies the name: Emerald Pools. They are situated in an isolated area and almost seem enchanted. A magical place.

➜ In Tramonti di Sopra, instead of turning in to the picnic area, go straight to the church and turn L, following the signs to the rock-climbing gym (Palestra di Roccia). Continue for 1km and leave the car near a bend on the R, at which point on the L you will see a gravel path. Follow it until you reach the pools, near a footbridge close to the river. If you go on further, there are more small pools and mini-canyons between the rocks.

30 mins easy, 46.3097, 12.7616

Torrente Palar

10

9

pools near a picnic area, and more further up the river **6**. The real gem in this valley is higher in the mountains, though. The Pozze Smeraldine (Emerald Pools) **7** are just a short walk away on a mountain path. Their clear water and the deep colour will leave you speechless.

Continuing 10km north, you will come out in the valley of the Tagliamento - a river that flows from the Alps to the Adriatic sea. The Cascata Plera has a mossy waterfall pool and is perfect on a really hot day **8**. On the road that leads to the Cascata Plera you may encounter some *casematte* (gun emplacements), part of the defence system of the Littorio Alpine Fortification, built by Mussolini in the build-up to World War II, and a reminder that this has always been a border area. The mountains acted as natural sentinels against any trespassers seeking the fertile Italian plains.

Before moving on, why not relax on the banks of the Lago di Cavazzo **9**, near the village of Interneppo, where there is a broad, grassy shore facing reed beds teeming with birdlife. It's a good spot for a picnic with friends and family.

Only a kilometre away, near Alesso, the Torrente Palar **10** forms several pools, perfect for a few hours cooling down on hot ▶

Cascate Plera

The Plera Falls and Cavazzo Lake

8 CASCATA PLERA

A high waterfall chute drops into a blue pool surrounded by greenery. Even on the hottest days, the air here is always fresh, with small droplets of water suspended in mid-air.

→ From the A23 exit at Carnia/Tolmezzo, take the SS52 towards Tolmezzo. Cross the bridge and before you get to Villa Santina, take the turn to Verzegnis/Invillino. Continue until you cross the bridge over the Tagliamento river and leave the car before the 180-degree turn. Take the dirt road and follow it, passing by the casemates (gun emplacements). Continue to the wooden bridge where you will see the waterfall.

20 mins easy, 46.3978, 12.9261

9 LAGO DI CAVAZZO

You will find a large park with grassed areas and picnic tables at the southern part of this lake. It is set among mountains and there are possibilities for all kinds of excursions.

A East shore

This beautiful grass-fringed shore on the east side, with a view of reed beds full of wildlife, is ideal for picnicking. Children can pass the time in the big playground, or why not rent a canoe.

→ From Tolmezzo, take the SR512 heading SE, past Cavazzo until you see the lake. There is a nice beach 1km after Interneppo. Then follow the coast to the south. Cross over a wooden bridge, and you will reach the park at the southern end of the lake.

1 min easy, 46.3224, 13.0728

B West shore

A beautiful pebble beach on the west side, sheltered by trees. Good campsite.

→ Continue along the SR512 and turn off at the sign 'Lago Tre Comuni'. Down the road there is a car park near a beach. Turn into Via del Brancs and then R towards Tolmezzo. Leave your car in the parking area in front of the campsite and walk over to the steps to the lake. Why not stay a night at the ▲ Campsite Lago 3 Comuni, in Alesso (Tel 0432 979 464).

1 min easy, 46.327, 13.0651

10 TORRENTE PALAR, ALESSO

This spot is appealing as it is just a few-hundred metres after the village square of Alesso. The banks look towards the mountain and there are emerald pools where the valley narrows. You will be dazzled by the bright colours of the surrounding greenery. This creek is very popular, especially the quiet lower pools.

→ Head for the village of Alesso (from Camping Lago, following signs for Tolmezzo, heading S). When you reach the village square, take the street between Bar della Posta and Bar Macan, then the first L and cross over the bridge. Park and retrace your steps, cross the bridge again and turn L. Continue until you reach the fountain and turn L. Follow the path 200m to the first pool. Further upriver (46.3180, 13.0397) is a pool into which you can dive from a height of 15m. Once past the weir, climbing up on the R, there are wilder, quieter and even more amazing pools (46.3189, 13.0376).

1 min easy, 46.3173, 13.0473

12

12

11

13 The mill at the beginning of the path

days. The first pools are located under weirs but, once past the highest dam, the stream reverts to wildness, creating some of the most amazing natural pools with large rocks for diving.

The Arzino Valley will take you back to the mountains, where the river, one of the few not yet dammed or tamed by man, provides some lovely corners of completely unspoilt nature. At its source, a couple of miles above the hamlet of Pozzis, the river begins its descent into a valley that soon becomes steep and rocky, and the waters form a sequence of pools and waterfalls. Cerdevol **12** is the most evocative place in the area, as swimming in the clear waters of this white, rocky canyon is a mystical experience.

If you like walking, you can hike along the Chiarzò Valley, from Campone to the abandoned village of Palcoda. Along the trail, which follows the bed of the river, you will be forced to splash through many fords and, to have a dip along the way, go as far as the narrow gorge which you will have to swim across.
A little further on, the river joins the waters of Rio Neri, at a point where pools and waterfalls create a particularly charming scene. Here a waterfall falls from a rock slide down to a little pool – diving in will be irresistible. It's an easy but lengthy excursion, which could be testing for little ones. However, there are plenty of stopping places along the way **13**.

11

L'Arzino and the Chiarzò

11 FORGARIA

The small pool here is fringed by a pretty pebble beach and there are many rocks suitable for diving. The spot is easy to reach, and the beach is well-placed for sunshine. The only disadvantage is that it quickly gets crowded. Going further up the river you will find some smaller pools.

➔ Head north on the SP1. After about 14km from Spilimbergo you come to Casiacco. Go past the church and turn R into the small road down the hill. Park just before the stone wall that goes down to the river.
1 min easy, 46.2251,12.9582

12 CERDEVOL

This white canyon has been expertly carved into shape by the river, which has incredibly clear and colourful waters. There is a quiet pool, a huge, slightly sloping rock to sunbathe on, and a pebble bank for the kids to play on. It is a beautiful and magical place that culminates in a gorge where the water

flows fast over a narrow chute of rock.
➔ Continuing N on the SP1 for 10km, you will come to the edge of Cerdevol. Leave your car in a layby on the R, marked by a wooden board stating 'Area Pic-Nic Curnila'. From here, walk down the path that leads to a lovely meander in the river.
4 mins easy, 46.2803, 12.938

13 CASCATA PALCODA, CAMPONE

The Palcoda waterfall is the most scenic point of this walk along the river. The first section forms a fairly broad river bed, between waterfalls and small pools. The further you walk, the more severe but interesting the landscape becomes, with large waterfalls and narrow gorges. If you are not afraid of getting your feet wet, the trail is not particularly difficult.
➔ Campone can be reached from Cerdevol via Clauzetto (SP55, SP57). Or from Meduno go along the SR552 heading N, following signs for Tramonti. After 8km, turn R onto the SP57 towards Campone. Once in Campone, turn L in Via Centro, towards the Bar Strias. Follow the road to

a small square, where you can park. Then head down to the cobbled street between two houses and continue to the bridge, where there is a pretty mill. The path begins before the bridge on the L; follow it along. After a few hundred metres you will reach the bed of the river, at which point you will have to go from one ford to another. You will find blue arrows on the rocks, but keep your eyes peeled, as they are not always easy to see.
90 mins moderate, 46.2816, 12.8401

Lombardy & Trentino

The region of the great lakes, the Dolomites and fascinating valleys rich in greenery. These beautiful landscapes are perfect for trekking, having fun in the sun, or a dip in the water.

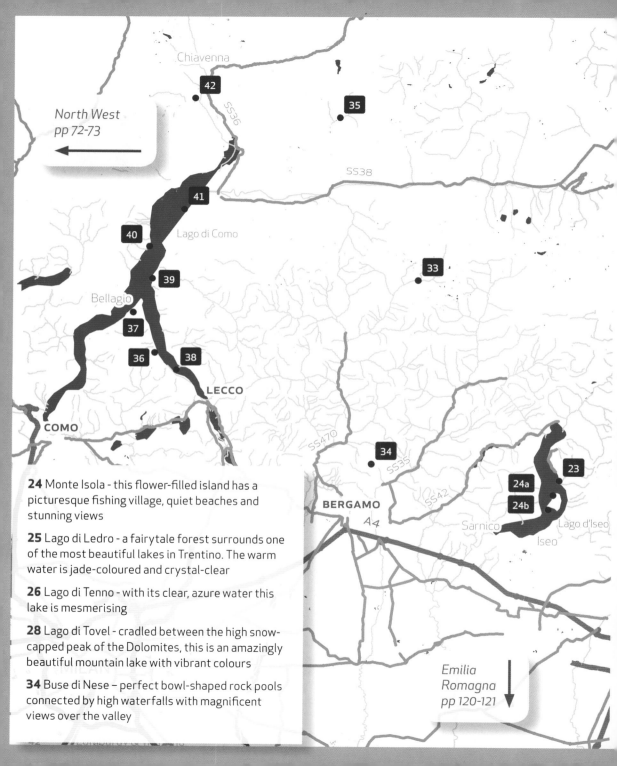

North West
pp 72-73
←

Chiavenna

42

35

SS36

SS38

41

40

Lago di Como

39

33

Bellagio

37

36   **38**

LECCO

COMO

SS470

34

SS35

24a

23

BERGAMO

A4

SS42

24b

Sarnico   Lago d'Iseo

Iseo

24 Monte Isola - this flower-filled island has a picturesque fishing village, quiet beaches and stunning views

25 Lago di Ledro - a fairytale forest surrounds one of the most beautiful lakes in Trentino. The warm water is jade-coloured and crystal-clear

26 Lago di Tenno - with its clear, azure water this lake is mesmerising

28 Lago di Tovel - cradled between the high snow-capped peak of the Dolomites, this is an amazingly beautiful mountain lake with vibrant colours

34 Buse di Nese – perfect bowl-shaped rock pools connected by high waterfalls with magnificent views over the valley

Emilia Romagna
pp 120-121
↓

Highlights
Lombardy & Trentino

Our favourites include:

14 Spiaggia Giamaica e Lido delle Bionde- in front of the magnificent Roman Villa di Catullo a large white slab of rock emerges from the crystal clear water of the lake

15 Spiaggia della rocca di Manerba - under the hill of the fortress of Manerba, one of the most secluded beaches on the lake, in a beautiful, unexpectedly wild environment

19 Torrente San Michele – from the lake shore a deep canyon cuts up into the heart of the mountain, revealing magnificent blue pools and high waterfalls

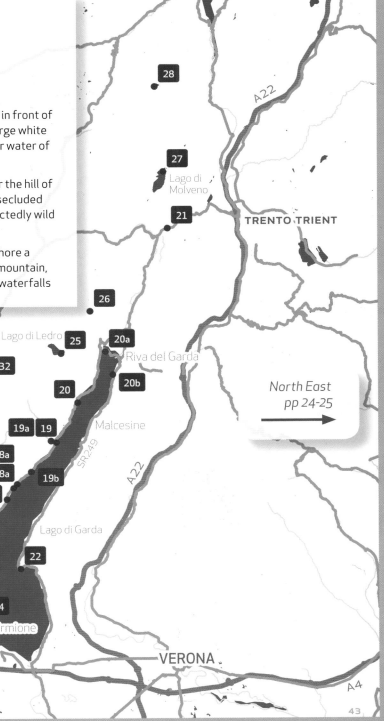

28

27

Lago di Molveno

21

TRENTO TRIENT

A22

26

Lago di Ledro

25

20a

Riva del Garda

32

20

20b

North East
pp 24-25 →

30

19a 19

Malcesine

31

29

Lago d'Idro

SR249

18a

18a

19b

A22

17

16

Salò

Lago di Garda

22

15

14

BRESCIA

A4

Sirmione

VERONA

A4

SS237

14 Rocca di Sirmione

Lombardy and Trentino Alto Adige embrace the famous 'Great Lakes' region of Italy, but also other landscapes, from the plains in the fertile Po Valle to the jagged Alps and magnificent peaks of the Dolomites.

In the centre there are hills covered with prestigious vineyards and picturesque villages, but best of all are is wonderful chain of sparkling lakes that run through the valleys and landscape. The stunning blue Lago di Garda is the most beautiful among them. Its open southern shore lies between gentle morainic hills planted with vines and olive trees. From the mid-point onwards the lake narrows quickly; the hills become mountains and there are dramatic vistas from the sometimes precarious lakeshore road.

In spring and summer, the coastal roads tend to become increasingly congested, and the beautiful villages on its banks ▶

Spiaggia della Rocca di Manerba

Lake Garda - South West

14 SPIAGGIA GIAMAICA & LIDO DI BIONDE

When the lake level is lower in the summer, large slabs of sandstone emerge from the lake, creating a beautiful smooth white rock beach surrounded by crystal-clear waters. Behind it is the famous Roman villa 'Grotte di Catullo'. if the lake level allows you can walk around to Lido di Bionde: a beach with a pier, a small bar and a magnificent lawn shaded by olive trees.

→ Leave the A4 at the Sirmione exit, and follow signs for Sirmione and then Terme di Catullo. 3km after leaving Via Brescia, park and walk over the bridge by the castle. Go straight ahead, following signs for the spa centre, Aquaria. Pass the Hotel Continental (do not take the road up the hill) to the end of Punta Staffalo, reaching the coast. Follow the shoreline as far as you can to the N. Lido di Biondi is to the R, about 300m along the shore. The Lido can be reached more easily by turning R before Aquaria. 🍴 Lido di Bionde (Tel 45.4994, 10.6074).

20 mins easy, 45.5027, 10.6063

15 SPIAGGIA DELLA ROCCA DI MANERBA

Beautiful pebble beach under a white cliff, above which stands a fortress. The walk there is interesting: first you enter a forest and then up a charming hillside with stunning views of the lake. The water is a magnificent green-blue colour and the forest provides shelter from the sun. It is also common to see hawks soaring near the cliffs.

→ From Manerba (off SP572 to Salò), follow signs towards the harbour of Porto di Dusano, via Montinelle. Before descending into the port, and at a R bend, see sign-board 'Comune Manerba' and turn L into Via San Giorgio. Continue on Via Agello to the car park at the end. Walk down the dirt road and follow signs to the beach. There are more small coves and beaches nearby, among olive groves. Nearby there is a naturist beach - so be prepared for possible nudity!

30 mins easy, 45.5568, 10.5781

16 VALLE DELLE CARTIERE

A magnificent series of natural pools situated in a small canyon with warm-coloured rocks: not easy to access. Upstream, near the ruins of a paper mill, other quieter pools are easily accessible. It is a great place to explore - follow the paths downstream for more pools.

→ From Manerba, follow signs for Salò and then take the Gardesana, the W coastal road (SS45bis). Enter Toscolano-Maderno and turn L after the bridge over the river (direction Gaino) and after 300m, as the road ascends, follow sign for Valle delle Cartiere on L. Continue to parking (400m) and follow the path up river 700m to the second bridge. Beyond are many pools and before a house you will find a path that leads down to an old concrete bridge with pool. There is also a small beach back down on the lake shore in the shade of ancient olive trees at 45.6440, 10.6191 with a 🍴 bar/restaurant. (Back in the village, heading NE on the main road, turn R just before the church).

30 mins moderate, 45.6549, 10.6082

15

Valle delle Cartiere

18B

17

are crowded with tourists, but there are still hidden beaches where you will find the authentic flavours of this Italian lake.

The picturesque village of Sirmione, for example, is famous for its Roman and medieval remains, with the striking Scaliger castle as a popular tourist destination, but it also hides a very special beach just below the remains of the fascinating Grotte di Catullo. The swim at Giamaica has smooth rock slabs, and further round you will find the the Lido di Bionde with crystal-clear waters, a pontoon and magnificent views **14**.

Below the ruins of a fortress, you will find the white rocky spurs of Manerba and the Spiaggia della Rocca di Manerba: a fantastic beach, surrounded by an evergreen forest and flowering meadows **15**.

The ancient villas on the west coast, including the eccentric hillside estate of Il Vittoriale degli Italiani, lead us to the town of Toscolano in the Valle delle Cartiere, along old industrial areas now taken over by nature. Here, the river glides through orange-coloured rocks creating pools interspersed with waterfalls, some good for jumping **16**.

Continuing north, the lake narrows, mountains become taller, the wind increases and picturesque villages such as Bogliaco **17** ▶

Lake Garda - West

17 BOGLIACO

A narrow shingle beach with an impressive hidden entrance. Beautiful hotel terrace.

➜ From Toscolano go N to Bogliaco and turn R at the Casa Cantoniera in via Bettoni. Cross the harbour and park on the L. Walk to the entrance of the beach between two narrow stone walls on your R, just before the gate of the restaurant. The 🅗 Hotel Bogliaco (Tel 0365 71404) has a wonderful terrace overlooking the lake. You must try their delicious Coregone, a typical freshwater fish from the lake.

1 min easy, 45.6728, 10.6529

18 LE FONTANELLE, GARGNANO

Le Fontanelle is a supervised lido beach with free access in the middle of an olive grove with lawns and benches. The beach is pebbly, but the view from the park is particularly pleasant.

➜ Arrive in Gargnano and turn R before the Hotel Meandro. Park your car and walk S to the village, along the road down to the lake. You will immediately see the olive grove and beach.

2 mins easy, 45.6912, 10.6687

A La Piazzetta, Gargnano

A picturesque beach in the historic centre of the village, overlooking a small square

➜ From Le Fontanelle, above, go S along via Rimembranza and turn L into a small lane after the car park.

5 mins easy, 45.6888, 10.6662

19 TORRENTE SAN MICHELE

Gorges with small pools, waterfalls and large boulders from which to dive. Upstream, part of a high waterfall flows into a funnel of rock. Below, a beautiful blue pool and a small channel glistens in the warm sun.

➜ Follow the Gardesana (S45 bis) and take the exit for Campione del Garda, turning R from a tunnel - pay attention as the sign is not very visible. You can pay and park in one of the new parking areas and walk to the square. Cross the bridge over the stream and take the path on the R. After the bridge on the old road, keep to your R and walk along a stone wall towards the bed of the river.

40 min moderate, 45.7544, 10.7448

A Le Spiagge di Campione del Garda

Explore the village too; it is in a stunning location, on a small strip of land topped by huge walls of rock.

➜ Good beaches hidden among olive trees. Also follow the coast N, on the old coast road, and you will find stunning places from which to dive.

1 min easy , 45.7533, 10.7512

B Porto di Tignale

A narrow beach slightly hidden and therefore usually not too crowded. Walk a little way along the shore S to find a fun tree to dive from.

➜ 3.6km back S on the S45bis, and 2.2km before the turning for Tignale, turn L at the entrance to the tunnel and you will find the car park and beach.

1 min easy , 45.7277, 10.7180

19

19

20B

20B

20B

22

and Gargnano **18** seem squeezed between the mountains and the water. The old town with its narrow streets is charming and runs downhill towards the harbour where there is an attractive, pebbly lido, Le Fontanelle.

The western coastal road (S45 bis) provides beautiful views with mountains overlooking the calm waters. Visit Campione del Garda, a small town situated in the Alto Garda Bresciano Park. Campione has always been a favourite spot for wind and kite-surfers, but redevelopments in recent years have blurred its charm a little. However, you will find many beaches, and rock ledges for jumping and diving **19A**. Turning your back to the beach head for the river gorge of San Michele, where deep pools, waterfalls and narrow channels form an aquatic playground **19**.

It is worth taking the SP38 (signed Tignale) that leads from the lake to the green highlands of Tremosine, where the views are absolutely spectacular. The amazing road follows the back of the mountain, and then along a narrow and impressive gorge carved by the River Brasa. Churchill called it the Eight Wonder of the World and it featured in scenes from the James Bond movie, *Quantum of Solace*.

▶

22 Punta san Viglio

Lake Garda - North and East

20 LIMONE SUL GARDA

A large, well-looked after beach near the picturesque centre of this pretty village. It is lined with several 🍴 restaurants and 🛏 hotels. There aren't many trees, and it can get busy, but the water is a gorgeous colour and the scenery is beautiful.

➜ Once in Limone, coming from the S, turn R before the pizzeria Torcol, and follow the road to the harbour car par and park. Turn back slightly and to the L you will see the entrance to the beach. Another narrow beach (45.8063, 10.7905) is located further S, and is accessible from a small street next to the football pitch - just follow the signs.
2 mins easy, 45.8098,10.7936

A Riva del Garda

Relaxing area with an immaculate beach full of greenery and trees and equipped for all sorts of activities. A pleasant break after a visit to the village - the view of the lake is magnificent.

➜ From Limone (above) head N on the SS45 bis lake road about 10km and park on the road shortly after the entrance to the village. Explore the streets of this pretty town and visit the Museo Civico, which is well-signposted. Go eastwards along the shore of the lake until you cross a bridge over a canal and there you will find the beach.
15 mins easy, 45.8813,10.8479

B Spiaggia delle Lucertole

A fantastic rocky beach hidden under an enormous cliff overlooking the lake. Amazing views.

➜ From Riva del Garda head to Torbole and continue on the eastern Gardesana (SR249) S towards Malcesine. After 2km, and the second tunnel, there is a small car park. Park and walk back along the tunnel to find a path down to the beach.
5 mins easy, 45.8491,10.8622

21 LAGO DI TOBLINO

About 15 mins N of Garda this lake is enchanting. Surrounded by reeds and hills there is also a fairy tale castle that rises from the mists.

➜ From Riva del Garda continue for about 20km on the SS45bis heading to Trento, until you reach the lake. Pass the castle and park at the next turn.
1 min easy, 46.0575,10.9719

22 PUNTA SAN VIGILIO

A picturesque harbour with shoreside taverna, a long public beach and the beautiful olive-grove Baia delle Sirene park with pay beach and picnic areas. There is a romantic, relaxing atmosphere and unforgettable sunsets.

➜ Head S towards Garda along the eastern Gardesana (SR249). About 2km before Garda, at the L bend, Punta San Vigilio is signed on the R. Park and walk down the beautiful tree-lined avenue. On the R you will find Baia delle Sirene and its beach (payment before 6pm, free afterwards) and at the bottom to the L the harbour with 🍴 Taverna San Vigilio (Tel 045 7255190). Reach the free public beach by going down the stairs on the L and along the stone wall.
15 mins easy, 45.5742,10.6792

20A

20A

Monte Isola

24

23

Next head towards Trentino on the north side of the lake, and visit the village of Limone **20** and swim within sight of this picturesque town and relax among the green meadows of Riva del Garda **20A**.

Continuing around the top and down the eastern shores of Garda, stop at the Spiaggia delle Lucertole **20B** near the town of Torbole, before getting to the well-known historic town of Malcesine on the north-eastern side of the lake, in the region of Veneto. Enjoy the sunset from the Baia delle Sirene park and then have a drink at the harbour-side Taverna Punta San Vigilio; a nice way to end this incredible tour of the Lago di Garda **22**.

Not far from the northern shores of Lago di Garda there are several quieter little gems that are worth discovering. One of these is the tiny Lago di Tenno **26**, with its incredible turquoise water and enchanting charm. And don't forget the romantic and beautiful Lago di Ledro nestled among the mountains **25**.

West of Lago di Garda is Lago d'Iseo, on the border of Franciacorta, a stretch of vineyard hills that produce excellent wines. Here you will find many beaches to relax upon, such as the quiet Spiaggia di Marone on the eastern side of the lake **23**, where you will see views of Monte Isola, a small mountain island and Europe's largest island within a lake **24**. Monte Isola also has

Lake Iseo

23 SPIAGGIA DI MARONE

A small, quiet beach located in front of a beautiful historic villa that also is a library.

➔ Drive up the west coast road of Lake Iseo as far as Marone. Towards the end of the village you will find the library ('biblioteca') car park on your L, before a pedestrian crossing and small bridge, with directions to Monte Marone. Enter the car park and walk down the steps on the L. You can also get to the beach along the river, going down the stairs after the bridge. In Vello, 1 km further N along the shore, you can go for a walk on the old coastal road (now only open to cyclists and pedestrians) and enjoy the beautiful sunsets.

1 min easy, 45.7403, 10.0905

24 MONTE ISOLA

This small mountain island rises from the waters of Isola lake. There are no cars, and walking or riding a bike is a real pleasure. The island has a few small beaches on which to shelter from heat (and crowds) in summer. On the southern shore you'll find some meadows by the lakeshore, or in Serf, after Sensole, there is a lido beach. You can reach Monte Isola easily using the frequent ferries from Sulzano to Peschiera Maraglio.

A Spiaggia Punta, Monte Isola

This beautiful, quiet beach on Monte Isola has fantastic views of the island of Loreto.

➔ Once on the island at Peschiera Maraglio, head towards Carzano in the north-eastern corner. At the end of the village near the school, Umberto Maddalena, there are signs on the L to Canogola and to Porto Siviano. Keep going L and go down to and along the lake until you reach the chapel, where you will find directions to the beach 'La Punta'.

1.5 hrs easy, 45.7199, 10.0788

B Spiaggia Sèrf, Monte Isola

A pleasant grassy beach with wooden tables under the shade of olive trees. Not far from the landing of Sensole in the beautiful and picturesque south of the island. Many lovely walks.

➔ Coming from Peschiera continue to and through the medieval hamlet of Sensole. You will find a small road to the L towards Menzino. This road merges near the junction to the Castello Oldofredi. On the L there is a mule track that leads down to the lake. You can also reach the beach of Spi: follow the trail that goes up to Menzino and look for the steps on the L and walk down to the beach.

25 mins easy, 45.6994, 10.0695

Lago di Ledro

28

The incredible colour of Lago di Tenno

Lakes of Trentino

25 LAGO DI LEDRO

With shimmering turquoise waters and a beautiful valley setting this is one of the most beautiful lakes in the Trentino region. In Mezzolago there is a beach which is only accessible on foot. The opposite shore is quieter and Pur is the only beach with facilities. Exploring by canoe 🛶 is recommended.

→ From Riva del Garda, take the SS240 towards Molina. Once you reach the lake, go straight, past Molina and before reaching Mezzolago, you will find a car park with a wooden sign-board. Follow the path clearly visible from the car park. Molina is a small town famous for its mills, well worth exploring; and Pieve is a village on the north-west side of the lake with accommodation and facilities.
2 mins easy, 45.8791, 10.7605

26 LAGO DI TENNO

A small enchanted lake with incredible turquoise waters surrounded by green hills. The nearby campsite has lovely terraced pitches with great views.

→ From Riva del Garda take the SP421 towards Varone/Tenno. Exit Tenno and continue until you see a large parking area on the R. Here you will see signs for the lake. ⛺ Camping Lago di Tenno (Tel 0464 553257).
5 mins easy, 45.9385, 10.8185

27 LAGO DI MOLVENO

A charming lake surrounded by beautiful mountains with amazing views of the Brenta Dolomites and the Paganella mountains. There are meadows and trees along the shore and some bars and restaurants nearby. If you are looking for peace and quiet you can find more private beaches near the campsite, when the lake level is low. Or hire a canoe 🛶 and look for the perfect secret spot.

→ From Trento take the SS45bis W and carry on to Lago di Toblino (stop here to look at the beautiful castle in the middle of the lake). Continue on the SS237 until Villa Banale, then the SS421 R towards Molveno. In the village, turn L into Via Lungo Lago - a steep road downhill. Park and head to the lake. The campsite, ⛺ Camping Spiaggia

(Tel 0461 586978), is at the end of the road on the L, on the path that leads to the Roman bridge and a waterfall.
3 mins easy, 46.1380, 10.9634

28 LAGO DI TOVEL

You will find this lake well off any main road at the end of a dead-end mountain lane. It is surrounded by fir trees, with crystal-clear, emerald waters and plenty of shade. Until the 1960s it was internationally famous for its bright red waters, due to the proliferation of an alga, Glenodinium sanguineum.

→ From Trento, head N and then take the SS43 and SP73 to Tuenno. From here follow signs to the lake. In the summer you will have to park at a distance and walk, or take a shuttle. During low season you can park 1km from the lake and proceed to a path on the L along the river.
15 mins easy, 46.2589, 10.9473

Vesta

Lake Idro

29 VESTA

The east coast of the lake Idro is steep, wild and sometimes inaccessible. Towards Vesta you can find several small beaches along the road. The largest one is in the village itself, just below the mountain, where the road ends. At sunset the beach in Vantone, near the campsite Rio Vantone, is also excellent.

→ From Brescia, head to Rezzato then N on SS45bis. In Villanuova sul Clisi, take the SS237 towards Sabbio Chiese and continue to Idro. After the dam, turn R and follow the signs to Idro. After the second bridge, take the second turning on the L and go straight ahead toward Vesta. Just before reaching Vesta, you will find the ▲ campsite Rio Vantone (Tel 0365 83125).

1 min easy, 45.7801, 10.5224

30 BAITONI

Perhaps the most beautiful beach of this lake, wide and sunny, next to a stretch of protected marsh with hides where you can watch a wide variety of birdlife. It is a quiet place with two ⊞ bars and a nice campsite.

→ From at Ponte Caffaro turn towards Baitoni after the bridge that marks the border between Lombardia and Trentino. Continue straight, cross another bridge and turn R. Park in the car park before the ▲campsite (Tel 0465 299 284). There is a path from here to the nature reserve. Follow the path until you reach a road and continue to the beach on your L.

10 mins easy, 45.8045, 10.5294

31 ANFO

A grassy lake beach away from the road and traffic, with a beautiful view of the fortress, built on the Monte Censo.

→ Exit the SS237 at Anfo roundabout take the first exit, turn L at the first intersection and park at the end of the road.

2 mins easy, 45.7625, 10.4951

32 CASCATA DEL PALVICO

A picturesque waterfall with a small blue pool at its foot. An ideal stopover between Lago d'Idro and Lago di Ledro.

→ From Storo, N of Lake Idro, take the SS240 NE towards Molina di Ledro. After 5km, park in the layby on the R, before the bridge over the Torrente Palvico. Cross the bridge and you will find the path that leads to the waterfall next to the abandoned house on the L.

2 mins easy, 45.8435,10.6207

34 Buse di Nese

34

several villages to explore. To get to the island you can hop on one of the frequent ferries between Sulzano, on the mainland, and Peschiera Maraglio, on the island. From the town of Sarnico on Iseo it is possible to cover almost the entire coast of the lake, going from town to town.

Shrouded in mystery, with a fairy-tale castle, is Lago di Toblino **21** while at Lago di Tovel **28** you will be amazed at the colours. These clear waters were once bright blood red due to the proliferation of a native alga. The phenomenon suddenly ceased in the 1960s.

From the Lago di Molveno **27** you can enjoy magnificent views of the peaks of the Brenta Dolomites and of the Paganella mountains: 'The precious pearl in the most precious treasure', wrote the poet Fogazzaro to describe this little paradise. The picturesque village of Molveno, with mountain views, gentle slopes down to the lake, lush lawns and a tree-lined beach, is beguiling.

Not far from Trento, the Lago di Caldonazzo near the town of Santa Caterina, and Lago di Levico near the town of Tenna, are surrounded by the mountains of Lagorai, in a valley full of possibilities where you will find the striking 'Arte Sella', a beautiful display of natural sculptures in the woods.

▶

35 Val di Mello

Bergamasche and Mello Valleys

33 VAL SAMBRUZZA

A lush valley with several quiet pools and crystal-clear water. Further upstream more waterfalls and deep pools await but are more difficult to reach.

→ Exit the A4 in Bergamo and follow Val Brembana taking the SS470 up to Lenna. Exit at the village centre and take the SP2 for Branzi/Carona. 15km after Lenna, before entering Carona, turn L after the cemetery. Go to the first bend and leave your car. Walk towards Pagliari, up to a group of houses and go down to the river, over the footbridge, and continue upstream. To get to the falls, continue on the road that passes above the village, until you see a waterfall coming down from the L. Cross the bridge and take the path on the R. Go down to the picnic area and then towards the stream. Cross it and continue down towards the river. You will see a large waterfall below you with a large pool but it is a difficult climb back out. Upstream you will find more waterfalls and natural pools .

40 mins moderate, 46.0246, 9.8094

34 BUSE DI NESE

A wonderful set of smooth, deep pots, two to three metres deep, one above the other, connected by high waterfalls. Enjoy the spectacular views.

→ From Bergamo head towards the centre of Azzano Lombardo, then on Via Provinciale, at the roundabout take the first exit. Continue and turn L onto Via Europa. Go straight until the road becomes Via Lacca. Ignore the L turning on Via Lacca, and continue straight (still on Via Lacca). The road will soon become Via Bracc. Continue until the road changes to Via Castello Monte di Nese. Continue for 5.5km, then park in Burro on the turning. Walk along the dirt road and then take the road on the R that passes through some buildings. Take the path on the L before entering the forest. The first part of the trail is suitable for children; further along it becomes rough and sometimes hazardous.

35 mins moderate, 45.7625, 9.7194

35 VAL DI MELLO

A magnificent alpine valley with a magical landscape of snow-capped peaks that exceed 2300 metres. Here, the middle section of the Mello stream runs clear and cold, and forms deep pools with giant rocks like islands in the river bed. The Bidet della Contessa is the most beautiful pool. At the valley entrance there is also a waterfall that looks like a giant rock slide.

→ From Lake Como, take the SS38 that runs through Valtellina in the direction of Sondrio. Once at Morbegno, continue to Ardenno, where you take the SS404 L to San Martino. In town, follow the main road and after the bend to the L, take the small road Via Val di Mello, to the R. Continue to the car park that will be on your R. Park and then walk straight ahead. After the first 3 minutes of your walk you will find a big waterfall on your L (46.2519, 9.6373) but continue past to find more pools.

30 mins easy, 46.2544, 9.6528

38

36

37 Bellagio from Varenna

Moving north into the Alto Adige, there are many remote Alpine lakes to seek out. They are cold but beautiful and include Lago di Carezza with its rainbow reflections, the charming Lago di Braies with its morning mists and Lago di Resia with a bell tower that rises from the water, just a few metres from the shore.

Back south to milder climates, and less austere valleys, head towards Lago d'Idro, a stretch of water between the green mountains, ideal for water sports **29**. It is usually very quiet in the mornings and early afternoon, so a perfect time for swimming and canoeing. In the afternoon it gets windy, so this is when the windsurfers get on their boards. The beach in the nearby town of Vesta is good and there is a campsite closeby. Another beach with a campsite, in the village of Baitoni, is Spiaggia di Baitoni, probably the most beautiful beach on this lake **30**.

Continue west to explore the valleys of Bergamo, beginning with Val Brembana, then to one of its diagonal valleys: the green Val Sambruzza **33**, where gentle meadows soon give way to waterfalls and tranquil, blue pools, surrounded by a forest of fir trees. A little further south, Buse di Nese **34** is abundant with waterfall 'steps' cascading from the mountain into this sunny valley. In Val di Mello, breath-taking alpine scenery surrounds yet more stunning pools, such as the Bidet of the Countess **35**.

Lake Como - South

36 BETWEEN ONNO & VASSENA

This stretch of the Lago di Como is wild and peaceful. The pebble beaches are protected by steep, bushy slopes. The road behind is usually quiet, except on summer weekends. Come in the morning to enjoy the sun as by later afternoon the shore is in shadow. This could be one of the most picturesque stretches of the coast, where you can still find some privacy, silence and a bit of mystery.

→ From Lecco, take the SS583 N, heading towards Bellagio. 1km after Onno you will find an open space to park on the R, which gives access to the beach. Along the way, there are other small beaches; those closest to the villages have amenities, like Pareo Beach, which has the ⊞ caffè Oliveto Lario (Tel 031 4449772), where you can find a good meal and hammocks to relax on.

1 min easy, 45.9192, 9.2894

37 BELLAGIO

Small public beach not far south from the historic centre of the picturesque village of Bellagio, beyond the beautiful gardens of Villa Melzi. You can also walk north to the tip of the headland to find the little harbour 'Punta' for jumping. The village is crowed during the summer and weekends, so visit on a weekday.

→ Reach Bellagio from the SS583. Between the village of Vergognese and Bellagio follow the directions for Porto Turistico/San Giovanni, to reach the beach. You can dive from the pier. The Campsite Clarke ▲ (Tel 031 951 325) is situated on the hills behind the village and is family-run and small, with a spectacular lake view. Or follow the signs for Punta, 500m north along the road from the ferry pier in Bellagio. There is a harbour here with walls for jumping and also a cafe ⊞ Punta spartivento, (Tel 031 951888).

1 min easy, 45.9771, 9.2470

38 ABBADIA LARIANA

Popular beach with a park where you can sunbathe, a miniclub for the kids and car park and a café. It offers a beautiful view of the steep slopes and cliffs of the Reserva Naturale Sasso Malascarpa on the opposite side.

→ From Lecco take the SS36 N and exit for Varenna/Abbadia Lariana. Keep L on Via Nazionale and after about 700m turn L towards Park Hotel Abbadia where you can park. You will find brown signs indicating the Parco Ulisse Guzzi. Just 500m to the N you can pitch your tent in the small ▲ Camping Spiaggia (Tel 0341 731621), and in the evening experience a typical meal in the ⊞ restaurant Il Vicolo (Tel 0341 700603).

3 mins easy, 45.8947, 9.3326

39

41

Lago di Como, less crowded than Lago di Garda, but deeper, longer and colder, is well-known for its majesty and is a must-visit. It offers one of the most beautiful views in Italy, framed by the Rhaetian Alps and the wild, green hills. You will find many villages to visit along its banks, with villas and amazing gardens - such as the famous Villa del Balbianello with cliffs dropping down to the water's edge. The towns of Varenna and Bellagio are two of its jewels.

Due to the mountains and steep shores you won't find too many beaches on Lago di Como, but there are quiet ones between Onno and Vassena 36. In the town of Santa Maria Rezzonico, in a picturesque bay shaded by a 13th century castle, you will find a pebble beach 40. And in the town of Piona there is also a quiet beach, surrounded by lawn and trees 41.

To end your visit to this region, we recommend heading north, leaving the lake behind to reach Gordona, in the province of Sondrio, where the Bodengo valley ends with the Cascata della Boggia 42. Here you will find waterfalls and deep rock pools at the edge of a narrow gorge. Not far away, the Acquafraggia waterfall is also spectacular.

Cascata della Boggia

39 VIA FERRATA, GITTANA

Suitable for the most adventurous, this informal *via ferrata* follows the cliffs above the lake and beneath the road. Excellent for diving and swimming in deep water.

➜ 2km north of Varenna, on the E shore, there is a sharp bend to the R at the end of the tunnel and room to park one car. Go down to the water's edge to find chains on the L, along the cliff below the road.

3 mins difficult, 46.0262, 9.2839

40 SPIAGGIA DI REZZONICO

Beautiful and secluded beach with a bay of white pebbles, shaded by a castle.

➜ N of Santa Maria, along the SS340dir, you'll arrive into the centre of Rezzonico. On the L of Castello Rezzonico you will find directions to the beach. Walk along the path to reach the beach.

5 mins easy, 46.0716, 9.2783

41 LAGHETTO DI PIONA

A beach covered with grass, overlooking a quiet bay with a beautiful row of tall maple trees behind. A pretty path runs around the bay to the picturesque Piona Abbey. Pleasant at sunset.

➜ Exit at Piona from SP36 and follow the signs to Colico on the SP72. Take the first L, then R and L again in Via Laghetto until the end of the road. You can park at the end of the road. Another grassy, tree-lined beach is located near a playground (46.1408, 9.3729), but is only accessible exiting Colico and taking the third exit at the roundabout with directions to the playground, and then following for the beach. Several campsites can be found near the beach. Ancient Piona Abbey is well worth visiting. The Abbey's shop has good wine, liqueurs, honey and other produce made in the monastery ⬛.

1 min easy, 46.1244, 9.3460

42 CASCATA DELLA BOGGIA

A picturesque waterfall that gushes into a large, shallow rock pool. This is the end of one of the most beautiful canyoning trails in the region: Val Bodengo. Pay for a ticket at one of the bars of Gordona and you can take the road towards Bodengo and find other pools within easy reach. The valley is also excellent for cycling. Not far away is the tall waterfall of Acquafraggia - a really spectacular sight to see.

➜ From Chiavenna, N of Lake Como, take the SP9 S. When at Gordona turn R and follow the brown signs for Cascata della Boggia. Continue along the road to the power station and park. A little further on you will see the path leading down to the pool. To reach the Acquafraggia waterfall, head N to Chiavenna and then to Piuro. Near the waterfall is a good campsite ⬛ in the woods, where you can find a pitch with a superb views (Tel 0343 36755).

1 min easy, 46.2817, 9.3668

North West

Blue lagoons of calm, clear water surrounded by the snow-capped peaks of the Alps; rivers flowing among the rocks, and waterfalls just waiting to be discovered.

Highlights
North West

Our favourites include:

46 Gole del Sesia - scramble and swim between high granite walls until you reach a large pool at the end of the gorges, an extraordinary experience

47 Ponte di Scopetta - an ancient Roman bridge with a small quiet pool is the perfect place to relax, while excitement awaits those who explore downstream

50 Rassa - a delightful village with a superb series of pools and waterfal

53 Torrente Fer - perfect emerald pools with huge rocks, close to a nice picnic area. Great for the family

55 Torrente Prouve - enjoy stunning views of the valley while wallowing in a magnificent rock bowl

57 Goja del Pis – a high wall of rock keeps this beautiful waterfall pool secluded, quiet and intimate

67 Cascata del Serpente - a deep, eerie valley carved into the rock, where water falls into shady pools

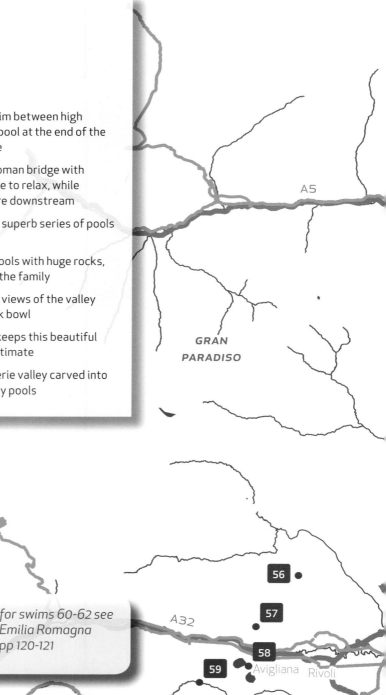

A5

GRAN
PARADISO

VANOISE
NATIONAL
PARK

for swims 60-62 see Emilia Romagna pp 120-121

A32

A32

56

57

58

59

Avigliana   Rivoli

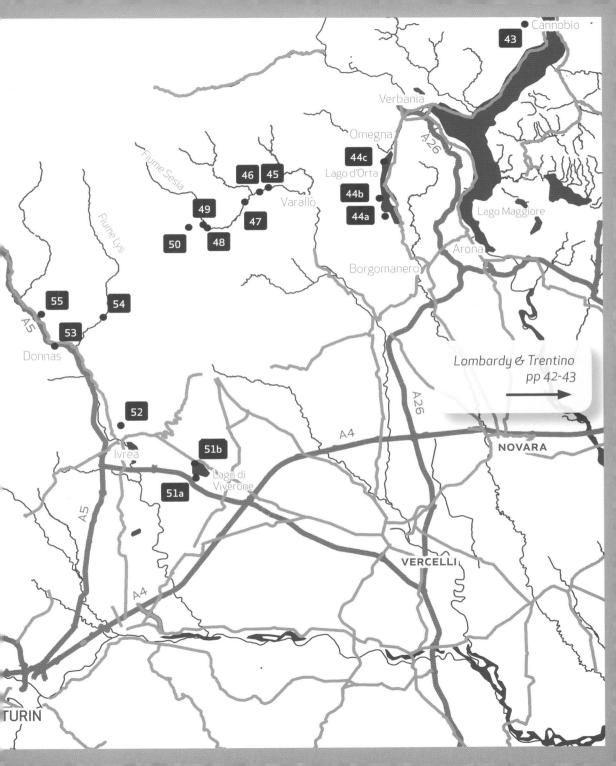

43 Cannobio

Verbania

Omegna

44c

A26

Lago d'Orta

44b

46 45

44a

Fiume Sesia

49

Varallo

47

50 48

Lago Maggiore

Arona

Borgomanero

Fiume Lys

55 54

53

Donnas

A5

Lombardy & Trentino
pp 42-43

NOVARA

52

A26

Ivrea

51b

A4

Lago di
Viverone

51a

A5

VERCELLI

A4

TURIN

44B

Descending rapidly from mountains to coast, it's far from simple to describe a region as diverse as the north-west of Italy. The region of Piedmont is cradled between the Alps and the Apennines, and framed by the rugged peaks of the Val d'Aosta. In these valleys you will find natural pools immersed in nature, and brightly-coloured, tranquil waters that flow between huge rocks and mysterious waterfalls. In the plains there are peaceful lakes, while the sunny Mediterranean coast of Liguria, with secluded inland waterfalls, also beckons.

Arriving in Piedmont from the east, from the shores of Lago Maggiore near Cannobio, seek out the the dark and mysterious ravine of Orrido di Sant'Anna, situated at the end of a beach with a beautiful, very deep pool **43**.

▶

Lake Maggiore and Lake Orta

43 ORRIDO DI SANT'ANNA

A beautiful dark natural pool, located at the end of a dark ravine, on top of which the small church of Saint Anne was built. Swimming in the narrow gorge, carved by the green rushing waters, is exciting. The pool is very deep - up to 14m - and used by scuba divers too. A little further downstream Camping Valle Romantica, the oldest campsite in Cannobio, has beautiful trees and gardens, and offers direct access to a pretty part of the river. The beach by Cannobio village has received several blue flags for the quality of its waters.

➜ Reach Cannobio via the SS34. Turn onto the SS631. Drive along for about 2.7km and turn R down a narrow road (brown sign indicating the orrido - the ravine). Park before the bridge. ▲ Camping Valle Romantica (Tel 0323 71249) is not far on the SS631.

1 min easy, 46.0603, 8.6692

44 LAGO D'ORTA

A charming lake surrounded by beautiful medieval villages, such as the romantic town of San Giulio d'Orta on San Giulio Island.

A Spiaggia Lagna

A gravelly beach, but with a pleasant shady grass area behind. There is also small pier to dive from.

➜ From Milan take the E62 towards Varese/Como/Chiasso, then take the exit A26/E62 towards Gravellona, and take the Arona exit. Bear L towards Borgomanero, and continue until you come to a large roundabout - take the first exit and follow the signs to the lake. Once in Gozzano, continue towards S.Maurizio d'Opaglio, and once in the village, follow for Pella/Lagna. 500m after the junction, turn L into via Pella. Continue for 600m to the car park and follow the signs for 'Percorso Lago'. Go around the small fishing pond, and in about 15 minutes you will be at the beach.

15 mins easy, 45.7840, 8.3977

B Cappella

A quiet, wild and unspoiled corner of the lake where you won't find many people. The slope down to the lake is a little steep and rocky.

➜ From Lagna, continue along Via Pella, past the town hall (municipio) and continue for 800m along the lake. Near a chapel you will see a parking area.

1 min moderate, 45.8106, 8.3863

C Spiaggia Boschina

Slightly secluded from the main beach of Omegna, this beach has a pretty backdrop; situated under trees and reeds. Its water is also extremely clean.

➜ Go back to the SP46 and head N in the direction of Omegna. Entering the village turn sharply R downhill before the bridge (Via Erbera) signed to the sports centre. At the first junction turn L into Via Fiumetta. Continue to a roundabout, then take the first exit onto Via Caduti di Bologna. Park in the large car park and head to the blue dome. Take the footpath on the R, then. cross the bridge.

3 mins easy, 45.8630, 8.3953

46

45

47

Passing the mountain of il Mottarone, head west towards Lago d'Orta **44**, and discover the small medieval town of San Giulio d' Orta on the island of San Giulio, a place that seems to have travelled back in time. Also visit the ancient town of Orta, one of the most beautiful in Italy. Near Pella, on the south-west side of the lake, there's a lovely grassy beach called Spiaggia Lagna - perfect for picnics and swimming **44A**. Continuing north there's another unspoilt place to dive and swim, near a small chapel **44B**, and on the north-western tip there is the beautiful, shaded beach of Spiaggia Boschina **44C**.

Next, leave the peaceful shores of the lake and head up into Valsesia, in the province of Vercelli, towards the Alps. Visit Varallo, a pleasant little town divided in two by the Mastallone stream and you should visit Isola **45**, where you will find two iridescent river pools - a prelude to the beauty that the valley has to offer. A few kilometers further on there's also Gola del Sesia - the gorges of Sesia - where the river runs between tall granite walls. This is a breathtaking place **46**. Further upstream, the Romanesque bridge of Scopetta is a popular place where the river flows between huge boulders and beaches **47**.

▶

Valsesia

45 LOCALITÀ ISOLA

A series of river pools near the village of Isola di Vocca, in a beautiful mountain setting. The first is deeper and located just below the bridge that leads to the town; while a short walk through the woods will bring you to the second one. Here you can choose whether to relax on the rocks in the sun, or on the soft grass in the shade. A little before, near the rafting centre, there is a long, quiet pool with a green lawn.

→ Head to Borgosesia and take the SP299 in the direction of Varallo. Pass the town, and after less than 9km, on the L you will find the signs for 'Sesia Rafting'. There's access to river pool here, if you cross the grass in front of the car park, but better to continue for 200m and turn L at the sign 'Loc. Isola'. Cross the bridge and there is parking on the L. On the R a path leads across the grass to a lovely, sheltered upstream pool, about 50m above the bridge. Or walk back to the bridge and you'll find a path down to the main pool, just beneath it. (For rafting activities the ⚑ Centro Rafting Sesia is Tel 348 005 3978 and organises outings on the river).
3 mins easy, 45.8269, 8.1719

46 GOLA DEL SESIA

The gorge of Sesia, which runs betwen tall narrow granite walls, is just a few feet wide. It reflects the rays of the sun in its turquoise water. The setting of this gorge is stunning. Dive in and swim in the gorge then swim downstream to reach the large pool.

→ 600m W of Località Isola, still on the SS299, you will find an open space on the L, and just below it a wooden sign-board. Leave your car and take one of the little paths leading down to the river.
2 mins easy, 45.8202, 8.1544

47 PONTE DI SCOPETTA

After a narrow stretch between granite rapids, the Sesia forms a quiet pool in the shade of the Roman bridge of Scopetta. You will find about 700m of beautiful and fascinating rapids, pools and waterfalls. Depending on the flow, the river could be dangerous, so be careful if swimming under the bridge and downstream.

→ 4km upstream of the Gola del Sesia, at the beginning of the town of Scopetta, leave your car on the L after the pedestrian crossing (there are wooden fences and an information kiosk). Follow the dirt road until you find the bridge. Not far from here you can pitch your tent at ▲ Campeggio ai Dinelli (Tel 0163 71517).
2 mins easy, 45.8058, 8.1261

46

48

49

Continuing upstream along the Valsesia, stop at Piode **48**, where you will find popular pools and some good food, and the side-valley of the River Sorba with dramatic waterfalls at the 'Blue Lagoon' **49**. Go up the valley to Rassa, an old-style village frozen in time with pools, waterfalls and fun water slides **50**.

Continuing along Valsesia you will arrive at the foot of Monte Rosa, the second-highest mountain in the Alps, and the highest in Switzerland. We recommend back-tracking along the valley and heading towards Canavese in the province of Turin, a region dotted with castles and monumental residences. On the way you will come to Lago Viverone with a wild shore full of lush greenery, situated in the morainic hills of Serra **51**. Or at Lago Sirio, where motor boats are forbidden and water quality is high, rent canoes and paddle boats **52**.

Follow the course of the river Dora Baltea; a tributary of the River Po, until you reach the beginning of the Val d'Aosta. This stunning valley is dotted with forts and castles and there are many wild, isolated side valleys, waiting to be discovered. The area is home to four of the highest Alpine peaks whose massive cliff faces loom above.

▶

50 Rassa

Sorba Valley

48 PIODE

Two popular pools formed by the river Sesia below the village. They are used by locals as a public swimming pool and - situated near the basketball courts - are also used by the team to cool down after a game. All around you will find small pebble beaches and lush grass, in a valley with stunning views.

→ Simply follow the SS299 for 8km W beyond Scopetta to reach Piode. Turn L onto the narrow bridge. Park after the basketball courts. You will see the pools and can easily get down to the river by passing the stone and wooden house at the end of the car park. Nearby, next to the river, the restaurant 🍴 Giardini (Tel 0163 71135) offers wonderful meals in a charming atmosphere. Or for some typical food of the area, cross over the river and try the restaurant 🍴 Pescatori (Tel 0163 71156) which has some great fish dishes for you to try.

1 min easy, 45.7704, 8.0504

49 LE LAGUNE BLU

A swimming pool carved into a rock, powered by a fast-flowing waterfall. But this is only a prelude of what awaits further up the river. Locals call it 'The Blue Lagoon' and soon you will understand why. The sun arrives late and leaves early; so it's best to visit around midday.

From the bridge over the Sesia at Piode (swim 48), walk along the small road (Via Ponte) upstream 300m until you reach another bridge over the stream. From there you can go down to the waterfall and pool or head further upstream. Going up river is not difficult; just be careful with the slippery rocks. In less than 15 minutes you will come to the large pool.

1 min easy, 45.7732, 8.0449

50 RASSA

A wonderful series of pools among smooth rocks, connected by waterfalls and water slides - all downstream from a beautiful village that seems to have changed little over time. A charming and curious place with stone houses overlooking the river Sorba. The surrounding mountains offer many possibilities for hiking.

→ Continue on NW past Piode on the SP299, and turn L, following signs for Rassa. Continue on the SP82 until you reach the entrance of the village, and park just after the bridge. Backtrack on foot, and on the R side of the bridge you will find a path down to the stream. Carry on down to find deeper pools and beautiful waterfalls. The light at sunset is something spectacular. After the sun goes down, stop at the 🍴 Hostaria di Bricai (Tel 0163 77264) and try out dishes with a mix of tradition and innovation.

1 min easy, 45.7695, 8.0169

Lago Sirio

51

52

Torrente Fer, near the forest of Cignas **53**, is a beautiful place. It is not difficult to understand why Camillo Benso, Count of Cavour, was devoted to this place: natural pools running between large, smooth rocks, where emerald waters flow from one waterfall to another, is reason enough! It is also a great place to go canyoning.

If you go up the river, you will see the beautiful view of the Fortress of Bard standing in front of you - a brilliant example of a military stronghold more than 200 years old. Heading up the Valle del Lys towards Monte Rosa there are breath-taking views of the Alps and the river Lys has bright-blue water, forming natural swimming pools surrounded by giant boulders **54**.

Under the castle of Arnad (an aristocratic residence dating back to the 14th century) a short path leads to some magnificent pools carved into the rock by the Torrente Prouve, where you bathe while enjoying the vista of the valley below **55**.

Continuing along the Aosta valley, the mountains become more impractical and the gorges and streams more difficult to reach. It is best to avoid the alpine lakes as they are

▶

Lake Viverone and Lake Sirio

51 LAGO DI VIVERONE

The Lago di Viverone is situated among peaceful green hills. Its east coast is very populated, and has many private beaches and promenades, although none of the small towns that surround it offer special attractions. The south and west shores are wild, however, and the lush greenery offers shelter and food to the many migratory birds.

A South west shore
A small secluded beach backed by a beautiful forest.

→ From Anzasco (on N end of lake) head E along the SP228 up to the roundabout (windsurfer sail in its middle) and turn R. After 1.5km bear L signed for campsite Haway. Depending on your car, decide whether to park at the campsite or drive along the dirt road beyond. You will find two trails on the R, both of which lead to small beaches. The campsite Camping Haway ▲ (Tel 0161 98403) is located at a short distance from the beach and is surrounded by woods with direct access to the lake.
1 min easy, 45.4068, 8.0287

B North shore
Campsite Plein Soleil has pitches right on the lake while other smaller beaches can be found through the woodland paths. The Bar Pizzeria Moresco has a small beach with a beautiful lawn.

→ From Anzasco head W on the SS228 but turn L after 200m onto a small road, following the signs for the ▲ campsite Plein Soleil (Tel 0125 72408) and the ⑪ Pizzeria Moresco.
1 min easy, 45.4279, 8.0261

52 LAGO SIRIO

A small, quiet lake in a green valley where the water is warm. Thanks to the ban on the use of motor boats the water is also crystal-clear. You can walk along the pedestrian path along the eastern shore, where there are picnic areas and small beaches. There are two resorts, one on the south-east shore and one on the east. Here you can rent beach loungers and deck chairs. The western shore is difficult to reach, except by the lake. A fun fact: the swan who swims around the lake is called Baldassarre, but he is not particularly friendly.

→ From the Ivrea ring-road, find Via Lago Sirio and continue 2km becoming the Via Panoramica above the lake. Before arriving at the restaurant Moia, just after the sign indicating you are leaving the town of Ivrea, you will see a small place on the R where you can park and go down to the lake. The ⚓ boat club 'Circolo Canottieri' on the south-east bank rents out canoes and paddle boats.
1 min easy, 45.4837, 7.8841

53

53

usually extremely cold, so head south towards warmer climes to explore the valleys around Turin.

The Lame di Varisella, on the Torrente Ceronda, is a splendid example of a pre-Alpine valley. This outdoor aquatic playground is great for kids, with pools and rocks to dive from and climb upon 56. Better for grown-ups is Goja del Pis, a 14 metre waterfall that plunges between steep walls of hard rock into a pool 30 metres in diameter 57. Less striking but equally enjoyable are the two Avigliana lakes 58.

Heading south, towards the barren Ligurian hills and mountains, visit Valle dell'Orba, or the beautiful pools of Canobio (not Cannobio, mentioned earlier) situated in a sunny bowl surrounded by colourful red rocks 60. Drive through the mountains and you will see the typical Ligurian landscape of high mountain peaks and valleys dropping down to the blue sea. At the Cascata del Serpente, near the town of Masone in the province of Genoa, there's a series of pools and waterfalls hidden between the trees 61. And only a few miles from the coast, Laghetti di Nervi is wonderful, a tiny deep pool with a swing and opportunities for a high dive 62.

Fiume Lys

Aosta Valley

53 TORRENTE FER

Beautiful natural pools with crystal-clear water, set in the midst of the beautiful forest of Cignas. A picnic area is not far from the first set of pools, but it does get crowded here on hot summer days. Walk for a few minutes to reach the upper pools where it is secluded and quiet. The large boulders that surround the pools allow you to dive or lie in the sun. A truly spectacular place.

➜ From Ivrea head N direction Aosta, leaving the A5/E25 at Pont-Saint-Martin. Take the SS26 L into Donnas and after 2km turn L down into Viale Lungodora 2000, which immediately goes under the railway. Continue 1km, under the motorway, and at the end turn L to the picnic area at Cignas. Park and follow the wooden fence, looking for an opening. You will find a path that will take you to the first set of pools. Continuing upstream, climbing over a big rock, you will soon find other natural pools and waterfalls.

3 mins easy, 45.5976, 7.7569

54 FIUME LYS

In the beautiful Valle del Lys, the river follows a difficult path around the large boulders that lie in its bed. Its light blue waters flow between the boulders, forming small pools and waterfalls. There are also a set of pools and natural water slides which are fun to ride on an lilo!

➜ From Pont-Saint-Martin (see above) head R away from Donnas on the SS26 and at the first roundabout (with the dome) bear L on the SR44 towards Gressoney, following the course of the river. After about 7km, pass Lillianes and 200m after the turning for the campsite you will find places to park. Other places are easily found further along the road. Below the ▲ Camping Mongenet (45.6374, 7.8480, Tel 0125 832391) there is a set of pools and natural water slides which are fun to ride on inflatables for a little DIY rafting adventure.

1 min easy, 45.6388, 7.8511

55 TORRENTE PROUVE

Below the Castle Arnad, a path leads to a huge block of rock where the river Prouve has carved out beautiful pools over the years. Here you will find natural swimming pools with breathtaking views.

➜ From Donnas, continue along the SS26. 3km after passing the huge complex of Fort Bard, take a small road on the R, following the sign for ⬛ 'Osteria L'Arcaden' (Tel 0125 966928, where you can try tasty snacks typical of the Aosta Valley). Just before the Osteria, turn L, then R immediately up a road signed Bonavesse. After the bridge over the river turn R again, towards Bonavesse-Vacheres. At the first bend to the R, take the small road uphill on the L until a hairpin turn to the R, where you will see a small clearing near the upper part of Arnad's Castle. Here there is space to park 3 or 4 cars. The path begins between the two stone walls.

12 mins moderate, 45.6434, 7.7312

53

53 Torrente Fer

56

56

58

57

Goja del Pis

The Valleys of Turin

56 TORRENTE CERONDA, VARISELLA

Two large turquoise pools, nestled between jagged rocks in the middle of a wild, natural valley. You can dive, climb, swim or sit quietly, enjoying the silence of the forest.

→ From Ivrea take the A5/E612 and then A55 towards Turin and exit at Borgaro, following direction towards Torino/Venaria Reale Nord. Continue about 14km N to bear L on the SP181 for Fiano. Take the SP182 towards Varisella and take the first exit at the roundabout. Follow Via Torino until the end, keep R until you see a small church on the R. Pass the car park and at the next parking space take the path down to the river.

5 mins easy, 45.2026, 7.4806

57 GOJA DEL PIS, VILLA DORA

A 14m waterfall that gushes through the rocks, falling into a natural swimming pool enclosed by high walls. Impressive and fun. A rope on the right-hand side will help you climb the wall, to then dive into the cool waters. Before reaching the waterfall, you will have to skirt along the Torrente Messa, which forms small pools interspersed with waterfalls.

→ From A32/E70 Avigliana Ovest head N (SP197) towards Almese. At the roundabout before the village, take the exit following Almese Centro/Rivra Milanere. After the church, turn R at the next intersection, over the river bridge and continue on uphill. Turn L into Via San Sebastiano after 200m and after about 1km you will see signs for the path to Goja del Pis. Leave your car between two tight turns and continue along the dirt road that, becomes a path.

15 mins easy, 45.1286, 7.3987

58 LAGHI DI AVIGLIANA

Overlooked by the morainic amphitheater of Rivoli-Avigliana, the two small lakes are surrounded by mountains. The smallest one is in a nature reserve so you cannot swim in it. However, a beautiful pebble beach is located on the north-west bank of the largest one, surrounded by trees and meadows. It is accessible from a cycling/pedestrian route.

→ From the A32/E70, exit at Avigliana Est and head 3km S, past Avigliana. Once between the two lakes, at the roundabout with the SS589, take the first exit towards Giaveno/Avigliana Centro. Continue N until the sanctuary of Madonna dei Laghi and turn immediately L. Come to a sharp bend to the R where you will find an open space on the L and a wooden sign-board. Continue along the pedestrian route to the beach.

5 mins easy, 45.0716, 7.3847

59 TORRENTE SANGONETTO

A set of small pools and waterfalls situated among white rocks. There is an industrial area downstream.

→ From Avigliana lakes head to Giaveno (SP190), then turn R near the church onto the SP192 towards Coazze. Just before Coazze turn L Via Sertorio, and then onto Via Montenero. Park near the 'Biglia Vetri', on your R. Walk down to the river.

1 min easy, 45.0474, 7.2898

59

59

56

61 Cascate del Serpente

Around Liguria

60 CANOBIO

Two beautiful river pools, one of which is almost 80m long, set in a wide gorge surrounded by red rocks. It is accessible on an old mule track. Wonderful views and a superb walk.

From A26 /E25 exit Ovada, follow direction for Molare. Once in Molare, turn L to take the SP205 to connect to the SP207, towards Olbicella. Once in Olbicella, go over the bridge and leave your car in Canobio, before the wood and iron bridge. Cross the rion bridge and then keep R, following the red marks. Walk past some ruins and take the blue-signed trail to the first pool.

10 mins easy, 44.5339, 8.5880

61 CASCATA DEL SERPENTE

Dark waterfalls and pools set in a narrow, deep valley carved between trees and rocks. Exquisitely beautiful when the sun shines.

→ From the A26/E25, take the exit then directions for Masone (SS456). After 200m, as you enter Masone, go R over the green bridge and turn L onto Via Volpara and climb the hill. At the top you will see the yellow signs for 'Cascata del Serpente'. Turn R down Via Cascata Serpente. Continue down this road, through the underpass. Keep going ahead about 600m to find a path on the R at the first hairpin (tricky parking). You will find waterfalls and pools along here, but the main waterfall is about 10 mins upstream. Or follow the road on, following the signs for the Cascata, and you will find a high panoramic point indicated by a wooden sign-board.

10 mins moderate, 44.4984, 8.7029

62 LAGHETTI DI NERVI

A tiny pool fed by a small waterfall, then larger deep emerald plunge pools a little further on. There is also high swing tied to the tree.

→ Exit the A12/E80 at Genova Nervi, and follow direction la Spezia and then direction Nervi. Continue E. In Nervi, leave the main road before the overpass; turn L into Via Guglielmo Oberdan and then turn into Via del Commercio on the L. At the next junction turn R, passing the graveyard (on the L). Take the steep road uphill to the new cemetery. Park 300m further along, along the stone wall, at the junction with Via Molinetti Nervi. Follow the small road for about 2km and you will arrive at the village of Molinetti, where you will find pools among olive groves. Go down to the stream, following the metal fence. If you take a L from the bridge you will get to the other streams. After a bend to the R, follow the yellow signs.

30 mins easy, 44.3974, 9.0515

Tuscany

Dip in blue thermal pools hidden within the hills. Walk among cypress trees and medieval villages. Swim in the lakes of the Apennines, surrounded by forests and mountains, with rivers flowing between volcanic rocks.

Emilia Romagna, pp 120-21
Tuscany Swims 73-78 ↑

Volterra

SR68

**BERIGNONE
NATURE RESERVE**

71b

71a

72b ●

72a ●

SR439

Highlights
Tuscany

Our favourites include:

64 Fosso Bianco - a white waterfall in the middle of a
lush forest, with hot blue pools to soak in

68 Quarciglione, Solaia - a very wild pool with big
rocks from which to jump and dive

70 Canaloni - amazing pools and waterfalls carved in
the volcanic rock in a remote nature reserve

71B Masso degli Specchi - a trek through the
nature reserve leads to one of the wildest and most
fascinating pools of the region

73 Candalla - an enchanted valley, where you can swim
among waterfalls, small canyons and ruins of old mills

74 Lago di Gramolazzo - beautiful views over the
Apuan Alps, with sandy beaches and grassy banks

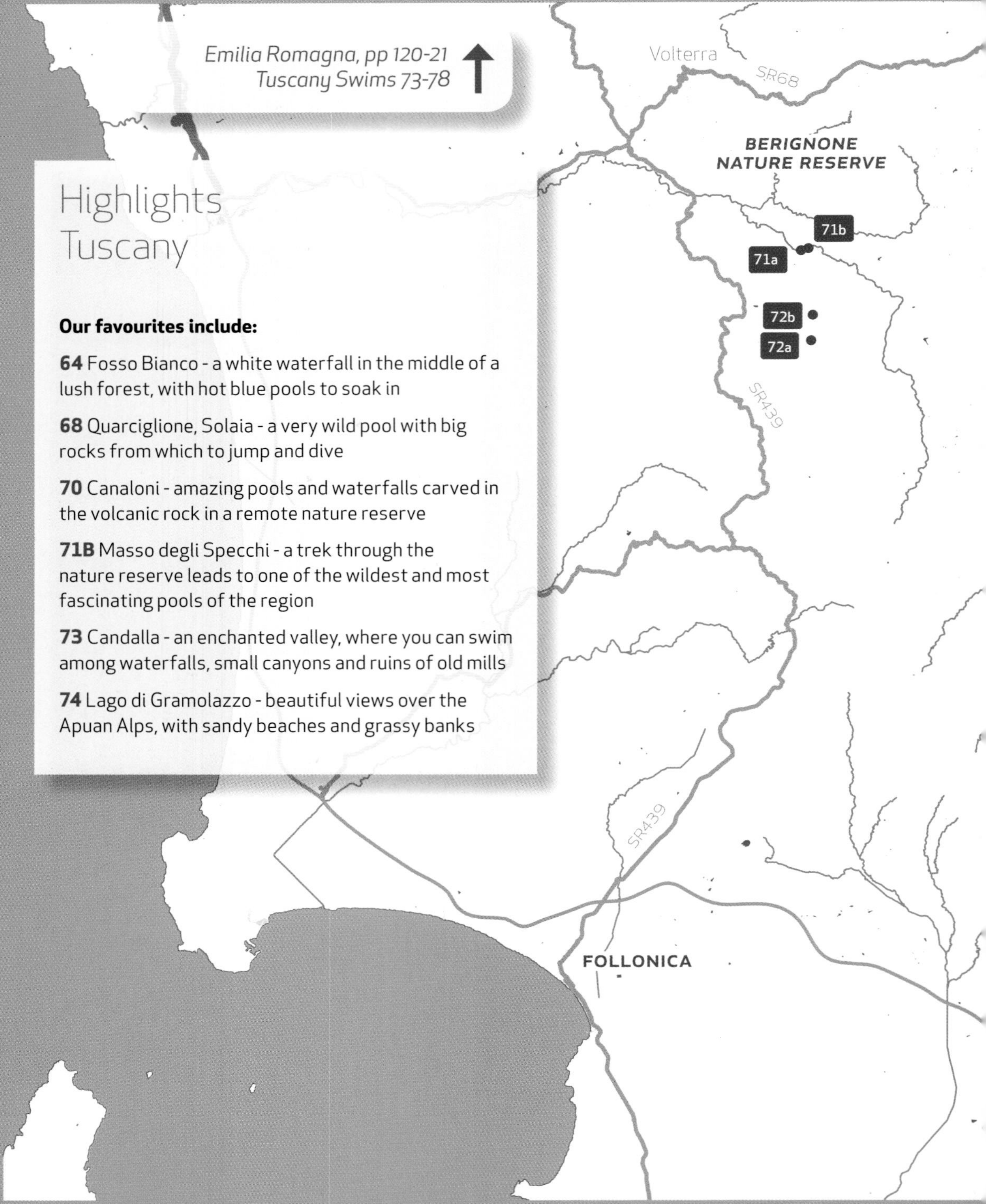

SR439

FOLLONICA

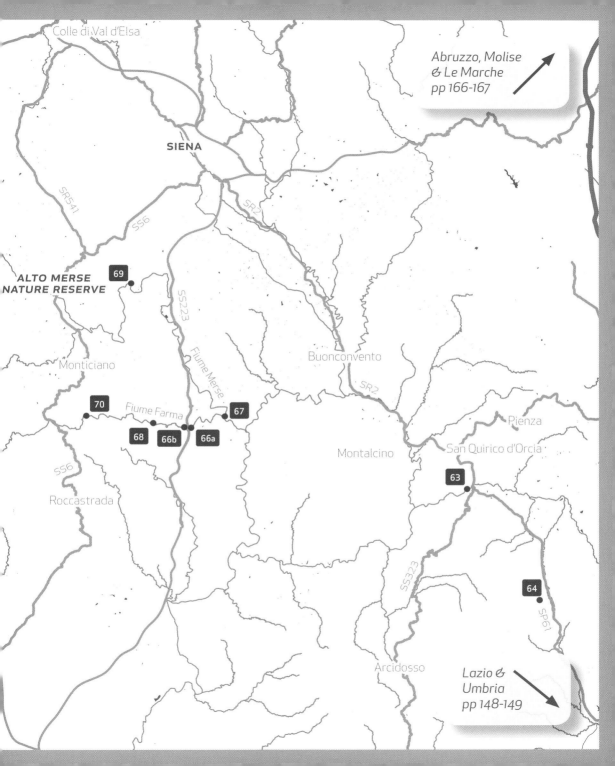

Colle di Val d'Elsa

SIENA

SR541

SS6

SR2

ALTO MERSE
NATURE RESERVE

69

SS223

Fiume Merse

Monticiano

Buonconvento

SR2

70

Fiume Farma

67

SS6

68   66b   66a

Montalcino

Pienza

San Quirico d'Orcia

63

Roccastrada

SS323

64

SP61

Arcidosso

Abruzzo, Molise
& Le Marche
pp 166-167

Lazio &
Umbria
pp 148-149

66A

65

Long, neat rows of Italian Cypress trees on the horizon and the hills changing colour from season to season; this is perhaps the most typical image of rural Tuscany, a place where nature has been forced to the needs of mankind with a grace that cannot be found anywhere else in the world. Yet this is only one of the many faces of this diverse region, where art and culture are submerged in the heritage of its great beauty. Lakes in the mountains, small canyons and wild, hot springs are the wallpaper to this place, with so much to offer its visitors.

To begin the tour of this region, you must start in Florence, the capital of the region, and visit its wonderful museums, or head south to the charming Piazza del Campo in Siena (regarded as one of Europe's greatest medieval squares) or west to the beautiful city of Lucca. Then, head for the Tuscan hills, forests and rivers and lose yourself in nature.

▶

Bagni di Petriole terme

Southern Tuscany's hot springs

63 BAGNO VIGNONI

Just below the village of Bagno Vignoni, a hot waterfall creates turquoise streams and small pools. A swimming pool collects water falling from the white calciferous rock wall. Plunge in and enjoy the thermal mud.

→ From the SS146 at San Quirico d'Orcia, head S to the village of Bagno Vignoni. Before reaching the village, about 200m after leaving the main road, take the dirt road on the L. Carry on for about another 200m to a clearing where you can park. The thermal baths are on the R.

1 min easy, 43.0258, 11.6197

64 FOSSO BIANCO, BAGNI SAN FILIPPO

The magnificent waterfall of La Balena Bianca (The White Whale), the azure-blue, hot pools, and the forest that surrounds Fosso Bianco (The White Stream) make this a magical place, in summer and winter.

→ Reach the village of Bagni San Filippo by taking the SP61 from Via Cassia (SR2). After leaving the main road, take the first

L. Head down the steep slope until you find a parking spot. Take the path following the brown signs for 'Fosso Bianco'. After a short walk downhill in the woods, you will reach the stream and pools. Continue on until you reach the waterfall.

5 mins easy, 42.9290, 11.7034

65 CASCATA DEL MULINO, SATURNIA

A beautiful thermal waterfall where series of natural pools have formed, arranged like terraces of blue and white jacuzzi pools. These are among the most famous Tuscan thermal pools, and for this reason they are always very crowded. We recommend you visit in the evening.

→ You can reach the hot springs of Saturnia from Pitigliano by leaving the village along the SR74 and heading W. Take the SP10 and follow signs to Saturnia until you reach the entrance of the Hotel Terme di Saturnia. Continue for about 200m and turn L towards the waterfall.

1 min easy, 42.6479, 11.5112

66 BAGNI DI PETRIOLO

A Terme, Fiume Farma

Thermal springs heat turquoise pools. Under the stone bridge there is a cool river pool in which you can dive after the hot baths.

→ Coming from Siena on the SS223, take the turning for Terme di Petriolo. After 3km you will find the Terme. Park on the street. After the Spa resort, you can easily walk down to the pools by taking the path between the road barriers. Other small pools are located before the resort and you can find a place to pitch your tent in the woods ▲.

1 min easy, 43.0794, 11.2999

B Upstream, Fiume Farma

If you feel like walking, go up the river from the woods. There is a meander with a large swimming pool and a rock for diving.

→ Head upstream, either in the river or through the woods, about 1km, passing under the road viaduct.

25 mins moderate, 43.0800, 11.2920

64 Fosso Bianco

Canaloni

69

69

Beginning with the region of Val d'Orcia, which extends from the hills south of Siena to Monte Amiata (a volcanic cone reaching 1,732 metres high), you will find typical Tuscan landscapes with vineyards and olive groves galore, though all art fans should head to the town of Pienza, the most important artistic area in the valley and considered the ideal Renaissance city.

On the top of the hills, there are several small medieval villages that are well worth visiting, such as the fairy-tale town Montalcino (22 kilometres west of Pienza on the S146). It is surrounded by a wall and dominated by an ancient castle and also well-known for its excellent wine (Brunello di Montalcino).

On a hill above Val d'Orcia there's the Bagno Vignoni **63**, which has always attracted travellers and pilgrims. The central square is home to a thermal spring tub pool from the 16th century, and its water vapours create a ghostly atmosphere against the Renaissance buildings. The water flows from the volcanic sulphur and calcium springs, pouring out onto a limestone cliff, and on its way forms rivulets, waterfalls and striking turquoise pools. A collection tank was built at the base of this cliff, where you can dive and relax. In the hills are some hidden mills that were once powered by the thermal waters all year round.

▶

70 Canaloni

The Farma and the Merse

67 CONFLUENZA FARMA-MERSE

A shallow pool at the meeting of the two rivers. There is a small sandy beach where you can stop and relax.

→ From Bagni di Petriolo (swim 66), head back across the bridge and up the hill. After 500m take the first L (small shrine in the middle of the junction). After 2km, follow the signs for the Agriturismo, turning L. At the following junction, leave your car and walk straight along the dirt road to arrive at the confluence of the two rivers.

5 mins easy, 43.0881, 11.3382

68 QUARCIGLIONE, SOLAIA

Two large, deep, emerald pools where you can dive and swim completely enfolded by a green forest. The first pool is surrounded by small beaches and has a small artificial springboard that you can dive from. If you walk on for about 100 metres along the river, you will get to more pools with wider beaches enclosed by large rocks. Great for those who love hiking.

→ Back on the SS223, head N across the viaduct and turn first L for the village of Lama. Cross the village S, in the direction of Solaia and after about 400m, at the junction, take the road on the R towards Quarciglione. After another 400m, after a sharp turning on the L, take a small road that branches off to the L (43.0936, 11.2461). Continue straight until you come to a clearing next to the river. The pools are located across the car park, hidden by the forest.

1-2 mins easy, 43.0834, 11.2561

69 FIUME MERSE, BRENNA

The river flows slowly here - ideal for a quiet day relaxing on the sandy shore. It is also very easy to reach. A great place for the kids to paddle.

→ From the SS223/E78 continue N again and take the L exit signed for Brenna, Orgia. After about 1km, turn L and go straight towards Brenna. Immediately after the village, park near the bridge over the Fiume Merse (43.2033, 11.2298). Cross the bridge and take the dirt road on the R that runs along the

river. In a few minutes you will reach the first beach. Continue until you find your preferred spot.

5 mins easy, 43.2054, 11.2303

70 CANALONI

A small canyon carved from volcanic rock, with a range of pools, beautiful waterfalls and breathtaking views, all in the middle of the protected forest Riserva Naturale Farma. You must not miss this place.

→ From Roccastrada head N on the SP157, in the direction of SS73 towards Torniella. 2km after the village of Torniella you will pass a bridge. Immediately after this, take the dirt road on the R that goes in the woods. Once in a flat clearing, leave your car (43.0834, 11.1419) and continue on foot for about 2 or 3km, following the red marks on the trees and the sound of waterfalls in the distance.

15 mins easy, 43.0898, 11.1785

68

Quarciglione - Solaia

71B

71B

71A

Nearby is the Fosso Bianco **64**, a small stream surrounded by a forest below the village of Bagni San Filippo, at the foot of Monte Amiata. Different sources of thermal waters merge in this stream, creating a beautiful and fascinating set of pastel blue pools held by the calciferous rock that makes this landscape magical. You will be amazed when you find the Balena Bianca (White Whale) waterfall in the middle of green forest, formed from a huge block of limestone from calcium carbonate sediments left by the milky mineral waters. Here you can climb, sunbathe or simply enjoy relaxing in the pools below. South of Monte Amiata there's the Parco Nazionale della Maremma, bordering the Ligurian and Tyrrhenian Seas, well worth a detour to explore.

Next, head south towards Pitigliano, an impressively situated town in the province of Grosseto, built entirely on a long ridge of tuff, a type of rock formed from volcanic ash. Stroll through its streets and squares, and at sunset visit the Spa town Saturnia (26 kilometres west on SS74) to see the Cascate del Mulino **65**. Enjoy the extraordinary beauty of this place, with its waterfalls and natural pools. However, it often gets busy here in the daytime, so it's best to enjoy the magic of this place after sunset, perhaps by moonlight under a starry night sky. ▶

West of Siena

71 RISERVA NATURALE DI BERIGNONE

The most spectacular stretch of the River Cecina crosses the natural reserve of the Riserva Naturale di Berignone. Among these gleaming hardwood forests, the bed of the river widens, creating beautiful pools between high cliffs - perfect for diving.

A Masso delle Fanciulle

Boulder of the Maidens. Emerald colour pools shaded by a huge rock. A place of legends.

→ Along the SR439 towards Pomarance, turn E immediately S of the bridge over the River Cecina (brown sign indicating Berignone-Tatti). After 6km the road turns R and begins to climb up the hill. On the L you will see a dirt road. Park here (43.3108, 10.9171) or continue on the dirt road up to a clearing where you can also park. Follow the road up to the ford of the river, which is usually dry in summer. Continue along a beautiful tree-lined path in the middle of the fields and you will reach a wood. Shortly you will get to the river - follow it upwards to get to the pools.

20 mins easy, 43.3044, 10.9344

B Masso degli Specchi

Boulder of Mirrors. A beautiful pool enclosed between two high cliffs that you can dive from. Shortly before, a small dam creates another pool.

→ Continuing along the river beyond Masso delle Fanciulle (above).

40 mins easy, 43.3054, 10.9396

72 TORRENTE PAVONE

Torrente Pavone (Peacock Stream) runs through a valley of dense greenery, where human presence seems very distant. It forms various natural pools between the igneous volcanic rocks.

A San Dalmazio

Pools of emerald water form in the narrow bends of the river. Easy to reach.

→ S from Pomarance, leave the SR439 to take the SP27. Follow it past San Dalmazio, and continue for another 2km, and near a 180-degree turn, go R (before you get to the bridge over the river) and park in the lay-bys on the side of the road (43.2553, 10.9439). From here take the path N through the trees. By following the river upstream, you will quickly reach the pools.

5 mins easy, 43.2560, 10.9415

B Montecastelli Pisano

This area is more challenging, but the descent down to the river from Montecastelli is spectacular. Here the path meets with the Cecina, passing by the old copper mines. On this route you will see many different landscapes; from long valleys where the river flows gently, to steep canyon walls full of waterfalls and giant boulders.

→ Continue 1km on the SP27 to Montecastelli and park near the church. Take the road downhill until you come to a crossroads. Take the road L towards 'La Cetina' (the old mine offices). Continue straight and follow the white and red signs of the path, and you will eventually arrive at the copper mine (open only by appointment). Once you get to the river, simply follow its course.

180 mins difficult, 43.2697, 10.9428

75A

73 Ruins of the old mill

The area south-east of Siena is a completely different Tuscany, made of thick forests of oak and chestnut trees where nature has been only marginally touched by man. In this region there are several nature reserves, within which two rivers flow, the Farma and the Merse. They offer several options for those looking for a place to cool down. Nearest to Siena, the Fiume Merse **69** offers the best places to swim. It's within the Riserva Naturale Alto Merse, near the town of Brenna. But our favourite river is the Farma river, to the south.

In the so-called area of Canaloni (Big Canals) **70**, the Farma is a young river and flows between volcanic rocks eroded by water and by time, to create a beautiful and evocative series of pools and waterfalls in a small canyon. The Canaloni can be reached through a pleasant walk in the woods.

About 7km downstream at Quarciglione in Solaia **68** the river flows peacefully, forming a beautiful, natural, emerald pool, adorned by smooth rocks and sandy beaches where you can sunbathe, and an artificial springboard to dive from. Follow the course of the river for a few minutes and you will arrive at another beautiful pool dominated by two giant boulders.

▶

Garfagnana, Northern Tuscany

73 CANDALLA, CAMAIORE

An area with many impressive pools, waterfalls and canyons. The pool below the mill is deep enough to jump into, from the top of the waterfall. Follow the trail to explore the river and ruins of the old mills. After a five minute walk, you will find the first set of pools. There is also a great place which serves food on terraces and balconies overlooking the river.

→ From Camaiore leave the SP1 to Casoli-Lombrici, and when near Lombrici turn to Candalla. Leave your car on the road before the mill, and continue on foot following the road that becomes a path. A great place to eat is 🍴 Osteria Candalla (Tel 0584 984381).

20 mins easy, 43.9571, 10.3238

74 LAGO DI GRAMOLAZZO

A beautiful lake in the Parco Naturale Alpi Apuane. The northern shore is easily accessible, with beautiful sandy beaches and grass. Suitable for families. The south shore is much more difficult to reach. There is a place where you can camp, with tent pitches on the lake and at the edge of the forest.

→ The lake is located in Gramolazzo and is reached by following the A12 N, then A15 (direction Parma), then take Aulla exit. Take the SS63 going E and just after Rometta, turn R towards Monzone, taking the SR445 and SP59 S to Minucciano. Carry on straight to the lake. You can reach the opposite bank by a path that starts off near the campsite 🏕 Lago Apuane (44.1599,10.2471, Tel 0583 1807364) The only other way across is by canoe.

1 min easy, 44.1632, 10.2470

75 LAGO DI VAGLI

A large reservoir that has the village of Fabbriche di Careggine submerged beneath its waters. The setting is lovely, with the small village of Vagli Sotto overlooking the lake.

A Località Bivio
A pebbly beach at the mouth of the river with a beautiful view of the village.

→ From Aulla, head E along the SS63 and when you reach Rometta, turn R towards Monzone, taking the SS445. Continue until you reach Camporgiano, then to Poggio, and take the SP50 R to Vagli. After about 8km you will be at the lake. Go to the first set of houses, turn L towards Vagli Sotto and L again to go down to the lake. A little further on, there is a free public swimming pool with a beautiful view of the lake and the surrounding mountains.

1 min easy, 44.1123, 10.2873

B South spur
Explore a wild beach where the tree-lined meadows at the edge of the forest makes the perfect backdrop.

→ Continue to Vagli Sotto (see above) and leave your car at the entrance of the village. Take the road that leads down to the lake and follow it to the bridge, cross it and turn R. Head towards the beach with the tree-lined meadows in front of you.

10 mins easy, 44.1087, 10.2941

Candalla

73

73

Further downstream you come to the Petriolo Terme **66A**, an ancient source of thermal water flowing at 43°, collected into shallow pools bordered by stones and arranged on several levels. Explore a little and you will find other small pools with thermal water and mud, and even places to pitch a tent for the night in the woods. There's also a cool river pool to swim in under the bridge. During hot summer days and weekends you will find the Terme crowded, so go there in the evening. Alternatively walk back upstream to find quieter pools, with rocks for diving **66B**.

Finally, downstream, at the end of its course, when the Fiume Farma flows into the river Merse, you'll find a shallow, natural pool near Agriturismo Val di Farma **67**. Here the river flows through the woods forming natural pools surrounded by sandy beaches.

Due west of Siena, in the province of Pisa, you can swim in the Riserva Naturale di Berignone. A picturesque, half-hour walk through fields and woods leads first to the famous Masso delle Fanciulle **71A**, where a large, solitary rock (Boulder of the Maidens) lies in the middle of this famous natural swimming pool on the river Cecina, surrounded by a pebbly beach. The name

▶

76 Lago Paduli

76 Hills of Tuscany

of this place dates back to an ancient legend about two girls who fell from the rock to escape the local squire.

Carry on walking along the river and you will arrive at Masso degli Specchi (Boulder of Mirrors), **71B** where two large rocks separated by a few metres create natural pools in a marvellous setting. The rocks are easy to climb, and the water is of various depths, offering many fun dives from different heights. A little further south (10 kilometres from Pomarance) a stretch of the Torrente Pavone winds between large rock walls, creating many enchanting emerald-green pools **72A**.

End your adventure between the Alps and the Apennines, in Northern Tuscany (130 kilometres north), in the historical regions of Lunigiana and Garfagnana. The jewel is Candalla **73**. Here, among ruins and fig-scented woodlands, the Rio Lombricese runs over beautiful waterfalls and between natural pools. There is a trail that starts from the old mill of Candalla, and slowly follows the stream. Take a leisurely dip, or swim in the small canyon. The trail will tempt you with many places where you can stop, dive and relax in the shade of the beautiful woods.

Continue north, 100 kilometres along the A12, towards the Parco Naturale Alpi Apuane. Here you will find a little gem nestled

▶

77B La Morra

76 LAGO PADULI

A lake with clear, pure waters, overlooked by Monte Malpasso. Fascinating trees grow on its gravel banks and green lawns. This place is otherwise very wild and barren.

A West shore

The western side of the lake is easily accessible from the SP74. Park in one of the places along the road.

➜ The lake is located on the Tosco-Emiliano border, on top of the Lagastrello Pass. The SP74 follows its west shore, and it is easily accessible from Aulla (A15/E33).

1 min easy, 44.3439, 10.1365

B East shore

The eastern side of the lake has gravel beaches backed by lush, green lawns. There are trees to shelter from the sun, or perhaps spend the night.

➜ A path starts from the NE corner of the lake and leads to the edge of the forest that surrounds the lake, where you can easily find a beach to swim from.

1 min easy, 44.3436, 10.1398

77 TORRENTE ENZA

After Lago Paduli, the Torrente Enza flows towards Emilia, crossing a valley of small villages. Here it creates pools mostly used by the locals.

A Selvanizza

A beautiful river that creates many swimming pools. The first is located in a sunny part of the valley, the latter at the foot of a steep cliff.

➜ From Lago Paduli (SP74) continue N and turn R on the SP68 towards Selvanizza (about 8km). Arriving in the village turn R opposite Bar EKO, towards Taviano. Cross the smaller bridge and turn immediately R by the orange shop/tavern to loop back towards the bridge. Take the dirt road and carry on untill you see an open space to park your car. Walk straight on to the river, which is on the L after a few minutes. Continue for another 10 mins to the final pool.

5 mins easy, 44.4430, 10.2518

B La Morra

Beautiful pools, gravel beaches and rocks to dive from. Go up the river for about 600m and you come to a narrow meander where it forms a natural pool in the shade of a rock wall. On the other bank there is a sandy beach, perfect for sunbathing.

➜ From Selvanizza, head on to Ranzano on the SP665, through the village, then turn R into 'La Morra'. Bear L and go down the street untill you find a parking space near an old barn. Walk to the river from here.

2 mins easy, 44.4579, 10.2667

78 TORRENTE BAGNONE

An emerald-coloured pool formed by the Torrente Bagnone, unusually shaped like a heart. It's not very big but it is surrounded by rocks which you can dive from. There's room between the trees to pitch a tent.

➜ From Aulla (A15/E33), take the SP26 N (direction Pontremoli). Once in Villafranca, pass the bridge and turn R signed Bagnone (dei Menhir). Take the SP29/SP28 up to the village. Turn L at the river bridge. Follow the signs for the sports centre (campo sportivo - second road on the L). Turn R at the roundabout and park after 200m. Take the path on the R side of the railings.

1 min easy, 44.3222, 9.9959

78 Torrente Bagnone, heart-shaped pool

Pitigliano

78

at the foot of the Monte Pisanino (the largest peak in the Alpi Apuane in Tuscany): the Lago di Gramolazzo **74**, a man-made lake with sandy banks and large, green open spaces where the kids can play. Some of the areas are equipped with wooden picnic tables. The opposite bank also hides some other small but charming beaches.

You should also visit the man-made lake, Lago di Vagli **75**, a large lake with the village of Fabbriche di Careggine submerged in its waters; and, 68 kilometres north (SP74), the clear Lago Paduli **76**, situtated in an extremely striking natural environment near the border of Emilia Romagna. Its waters are not deep, and on sunny days when it warms up quickly, a swim is heavenly.

Do also make time for the unusual heart-shaped, emerald pool on the Bagnone stream, with space to wild camp in the woods **78**. Further into the hills, you will also enjoy the many beautiful and secluded pools on the river Enza, with beaches for sunbathing and smooth rocks for diving **77**.

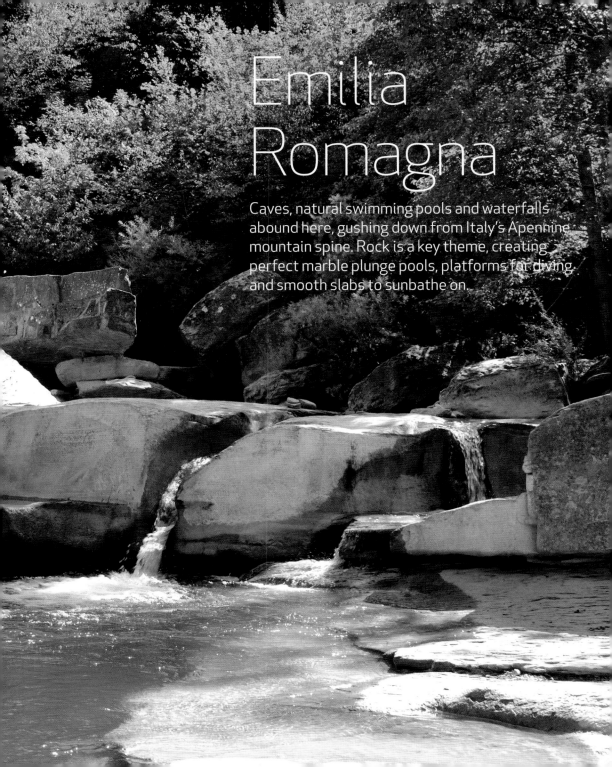

Emilia Romagna

Caves, natural swimming pools and waterfalls abound here, gushing down from Italy's Apennine mountain spine. Rock is a key theme, creating perfect marble plunge pools, platforms for diving and smooth slabs to sunbathe on.

Highlights
Emilia Romagna

Our favourites include:

80 Fiume Para - wild and known only by locals; many beautiful pools to discover, one after another

81 Cascata dell'Alferello - an impressive waterfall with a deep, dark bowl of rock from which the brave run and jump!

84 Grotta Urlante - under an old stone bridge a waterfall disappears in a spectacular chasm where the water roars. Some jump from the high ledge.

85 Bidente di Pietrapazza - a remote, magnificent valley, with natural pools and sunbathing rocks

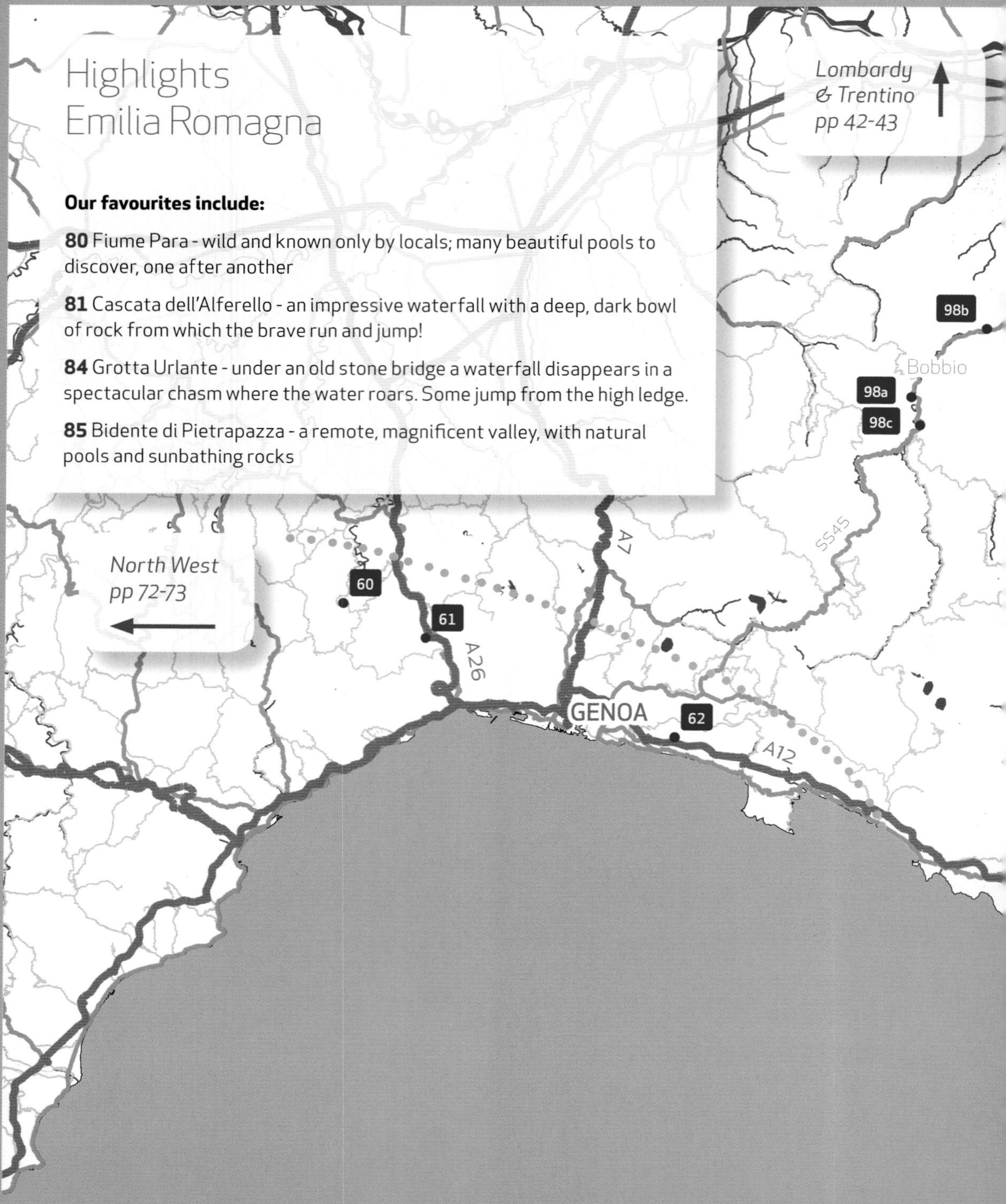

Lombardy & Trentino
pp 42-43

98b

Bobbio

98a

98c

SS45

North West
pp 72-73

60

61

A7

A26

GENOA

62

A12

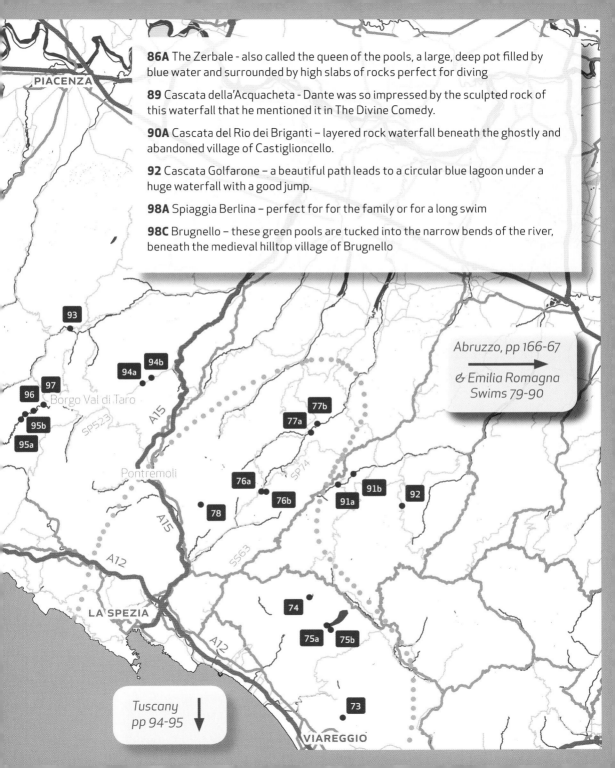

86A The Zerbale - also called the queen of the pools, a large, deep pot filled by blue water and surrounded by high slabs of rocks perfect for diving

89 Cascata della'Acquacheta - Dante was so impressed by the sculpted rock of this waterfall that he mentioned it in The Divine Comedy.

90A Cascata del Rio dei Briganti – layered rock waterfall beneath the ghostly and abandoned village of Castiglioncello.

92 Cascata Golfarone – a beautiful path leads to a circular blue lagoon under a huge waterfall with a good jump.

98A Spiaggia Berlina – perfect for for the family or for a long swim

98C Brugnello – these green pools are tucked into the narrow bends of the river, beneath the medieval hilltop village of Brugnello

Abruzzo, pp 166-67

& Emilia Romagna Swims 79-90

Tuscany pp 94-95

80

79

Away from its famous golden beaches on the Adriatic Riviera, you will find a very different side to the region of Emilia Romagna. The wild landscape of the Apennine mountain range rises up forming the spine of Italy, dividing the region from Tuscany to the west.

From wide plains, through rolling hills dotted with castles and fortresses, to high gorges and waterfalls beyond, this is a wild swimming paradise. Traversing the region from south-east to north-west, you will cross many valleys, many rarely visited, and skirt the national parks of the Foreste Casentinesi Forests, Monte Falterona and Campigna, and the Tuscan-Emilian Apennines, which together contain over half of Italy's biodiversity.

So leave behind Rimini and its crowded and noisy beaches behind, and begin this tour at the tiny country of San

▶

80 Fiume Para

Southern Emilia Romagna

79 FIUME MARECCHIA

Situated close to the rocky spur that is home to San Marino, the river Marecchia is an ideal place for a stopover or an afternoon with your family. The broad and constantly changing gravel bed of the river has little beaches, wide streams and pools galore. You will find improvised natural gazebos, tables and umbrellas and often there are stone mazes and natural art installations made by the locals. The valley is very open and sunny. In the surrounding countryside there are many beautiful places to explore on foot all day long.

→ From San Marino, take the SS258 as far as Pietracuta, follow the signs to the sports centre (after the car dealer GG Auto). Continue to the dirt road. After about 900m, park in the large open space and go down to the river from the small path. Here you will find wooden gazebos and tables. Go downstream for the large pool.

2 mins moderate, 43.9605, 12.3738

80 FIUME PARA

The Fiume Para flows in an almost untouched, steep-sided valley. To fully appreciate the beauty of the place, put on your aqua shoes or sandals and follow the river upstream, passing small waterfalls and gorges and splashing through the shallows. It's a pretty route with turquoise pools along the way. Not all sections are easy, and in some places you will have to swim, but it's great fun. Allow two hours for the full trip if you do the hike.

→ From Alfero (SP43), off the SS3bis/E45, follow signs for Mazzi (and Quarto) and then Para. After about 2km cross the (first) narrow bridge and park in a suitable place. From here you can go down to the river, to a small pool, and then river-hike upstream. Alternatively, take the first road to Pereto after the bridge and, after 1km on your R, you will find several laybys and a little lane (not easy to see) leading to the creek and many pools and waterfalls, just a few minutes either up or downstream.

15 mins moderate, 43.8549, 12.0918

81 CASCATA DELL'ALFERELLO

A short trail leads to the top of this waterfall where the Alferello stream flows over a leap of 32 metres and cascades down tiered rocks into a pool of delightful turquoise water. When it's lit by the sun, it is truly impressive. Nestled in a picturesque setting, the stream flows on for a dozen metres over smooth rocks, and then spills into an amazing deep pot into which it's great fun to jump and dive.

→ Just 1km from Fiume Para (swim 80). From Alfero, take the same road that leads to Mazzi, and after 1.3km you will find two hairpin turns. After 50m you will find a gravel car parking area (43.8488, 12.0722) and a signed path down to the L.

10 mins easy, 43.8517, 12.0733

81 Cascata dell'Alferello

82

83

83

Marino, the third smallest in Europe. Climb to the top of the fortress on Mount Titano with its magnificent far-reaching views and, in the valley below, shaded by the castles of Montebello, Torriana and Verucchio, flows the Fiume Marecchia **79**, meandering peacefully over a broad river bed, perfect for cooling off after a hot sunny day.

An hour away to the west lie crystal-clear waters and good hiking trails in the Para Valley, where the Fiume Para flows between high rock walls that are bathed in sunshine for much of the day **80**. Here an exciting swimming-walking trail follows the river upstream (the French call this an *aqua-randonée*). Finding the pools of clear, turquoise water at the end will make it all worthwhile.

Less than a kilometre away is the Cascata dell'Alferello **81**, a stunning 32 metre waterfall falling over marl and sandstone in stratified bands, typical of Romagna. Below the waterfall lies a beautiful pool that is not too deep, then a delightfully deep plunge pot, good for diving.

The Savio Valley runs parallel to the Para Valley and is more easily accessible thanks to the E45, which leads to the village of Quarto, in the municipality of Sarsina. Enjoy a dip in the semi-natural pools, or fish like the locals below the Lago di Quarto **82**.

▶

Central Romagna

82 VASCON DI QUARTO

Just below Lago di Quarto, the Fiume Savio forms semi-natural pools where many locals go to swim and fish. There is a large concrete dam and spillway but the swimming is fine.

→ From Alfero (see swim 80), head N and E to Quarto (SP43, SP113 then SS3bis). Pass the lake and the village and turn into Via Quarto Vecchio. Continue as far as the bridge, cross over and park. On the L there is a road leading to a pool. On the R, at the end of the bridge, climb over the guard rail and you can then go along the top of a wall that acts as a path. Follow it to reach several more pools of interest.
7 mins moderate, 43.8908, 12.0923

83 CASCATA DI CIVORIO

Here a high waterfall tumbles over a cliff and spills into emerald waters. All around there are tall, slender trees that create a perfect area for picnicking and snoozing.

→ From Quarto (swim 82) continue on the S3Bis/E45 to Sarsina, then the SP128 to Ranchio then SP95 to Civorio. Once in Civorio, pass the town, following the road downhill. After 300m, leave the car and take the path on the L, next to a wooden sign-board (43.9462, 12.0336).
5 mins easy, 43.9436, 12.0363

84 FIUME RABBI, PREMILCUORE

A Grotta Urlante

The 'Howling Cave', so called because of the loud rumble created by the plunging waterfall, is an extremely impressive site. By an old stone bridge, the river is engulfed in a spectacular, noisy chasm. The cave below has two pools deep enough to dive into from the rocks that surround them. Past the cave there is a pretty pool, which is also very deep. The more adventurous can dive in from the terrace that overlooks it. A magical and fun place to be.

→ S of the SS67 / Rocca San Casciano, on the SP25. The Grotta is located upstream, about 2km SW of Premilcuore. You will find a car park on your L. From there, take the road that leads to the bridge. To go down to the cave, look for a small path on the L, before the bridge.
5 mins easy, 43.9671, 11.7614

B Mulino della Sega and Ca' Ridolla

Beautiful blue water pools below high walls of rock and majestic waterfalls. A delightful site near a mill dating back to the 15th-16th century. There is also a great place nearby that serves food.

→ Cross the bridge at the Grotta Urlante, follow the old Florentine road for about 800m and turn L towards the river. Carry on, following the road and passing some stone buildings, then turn to the L to find more pools. ■ Agriturismo Ridolla (Tel. 0543 956829) offers great food in a lovely environment.
15 mins easy, 43.9716, 11.7666

84

84

86B

86B

Further north, towards central Emilia Romagna, you'll find a lush waterfall oasis, the Cascata di Civorio 83, where an emerald pool is surrounded by an amphitheatre of rock and slender trees, perfect for a siesta in the shade underneath.

Continuing north, you will come to the Fiume Rabbi near Premilcuore, where there's another magnificent natural feature: the Roaring Cave (Grotta Urlante) 84A. Next to a bridge dating from 1600, the river flows into the cave, making a distinctive roaring sound, hence its name. The cave, which is partially open, is home to two natural pools that merge into a third, bigger and more accessible one, into which you can dive from a considerable height.

Head back south a little, making your starting point the village of Santa Sofia. From here you can begin to appreciate the beauty of the Parco Nazionale Monte Falterona. Below is the Fiume Pietrapazza, a branch of the Fiume Bidente near Poggio alla Lastra 85, where over the years the river has carved out large slabs of rock, creating beautiful eddies and waterfalls. This unique place is well worth discovering.

15 kilometres north-east is the Bidente di Corniolo 86A, where you will discover the emerald Zerbale, also known as the 'queen of

85A Bidente di Pietrapazza

Pietrapazza and Corniolo, Santa Sofia

85 BIDENTE DI PIETRAPAZZA

The Fiume Pietrapazza, a tributary of the Fiume Bidente, flows through untamed woods with fabulous views. You will find many natural pools, with large boulders and slabs of rock for sunbathing and diving; a fantastic place.

A Upstream of the bridge

Small waterfalls descend between large boulders into lovely pools. You will find smooth slabs of rock where you can sleep in the sun.

→ From Santa Sofia, continue to Bagno di Romagna on the SP26, and after about 1.5km, turn R to Poggio Lastra. Pass the village and continue until you cross the stream over the bridge by the old mill. Park at 43.8836, 11.9001.

1 mins easy, 43.8838, 11.8993

B Downstream of the bridge

A deep whirlpool of blue water collects just below a waterfall, followed by a rock slide that leads to a smaller and a longer pool. It is shaded by two high walls of rock. Wonderful.

→ Turn back from the upstream swim

(85A) and cross back over the bridge, and after a few minutes, park in the second rough layby on the R. You will see a small gravel path ahead on your R. Park at 43.8891, 11.9017

2 mins moderate, 43.8890, 11.9024

C Mulino di Culmolle

This beautiful, natural pool lies just below the bank of the river. Downstream towards the bridge the rocky layers of the river bed have created striking formations.

→ Heading into Poggio Lastra, when you arrived, the fork up to the L leads to the farm 🍴 Agriturismo Mulino di Culmolle and arrives at a bridge. Leave your car and head upstream. (Tel 0543 913039, Why not book yourself a room here, or enjoy a nice lunch)?

2 mins easy, 43.9015, 11.9137

86 BIDENTE DI CORNIOLO

A The Zerbale

This place is often called the 'queen of pools', as you can dive from a height

of 13 metres into the clear waters of the Fiume Bidente. It is in a wild environment with large slabs of rock. Beautiful waterfalls and tumbling water slides.

→ From Santa Sofia head out on the Viale Roma (SP310) SW towards Berleta. After 8.5km, and after a sharp turn to the R, you will find a number of laybys for parking. A steep path leads to the river. To get to the most beautiful pools, wade across the river and head downstream before walking through the woods and then onwards to the rocks.

5 mins moderate, 43.9193, 11.8433

B Downstream from the Zerbale

Further down the river you will find several more pools, smaller and less scenic but usually quieter on busy days.

→ You can park near a hairpin bend, where there is a house, about 500m back along the road from the Zerbale. Behind the guard rail, a path leads to the river.

5 mins easy, 43.9225, 11.8467

85A Bidente di Pietrapazza

86A The Zerbale, 'Queen of Pools'

88A

89

pools'. Framed between huge plates of sandstone and marl, the view is stunning. You can dive from the high rocks, up to 13 metres above the water, but can also sunbathe comfortably on the slabs.

Continuing your journey, you will come to the magnificent Parco Nazionale delle Foreste Casentinesi, where it is worth spending a few days simply exploring different paths. The careful preservation of these forests, carried out initially by monastic settlements, has encouraged the conservation of some really interesting habitats: woods of beech, fir and chestnut. It is also home to a wide variety of wild animal and bird species, including wolves and golden eagles.

Over in the valley of the Fiume Montone, you will encounter another waterfall, the Cascata della Brusia **87**, situated by a medieval bridge and a great place for diving. Upstream are more pools in the meanders of the gorges, accessible by tracks down from the SP67 that follows its course **88A, 88B**.

Keep going and you will reach San Benedetto in Alpe. It's worth stopping here to trek to the Cascata dell'Acquacheta **89**, once praised by the poet Dante for its beauty. This 70 metre waterfall, which spills over a great wall of sandstone, can almost dry up in summer, so continue on the trail a few minutes to the foot of the Lavane Waterfall, where you can always swim.

▶

Fiume Montone and the Acquacheta Falls

87 CASCATA DELLA BRUSIA

Water flows over stratified rocks. A hump-back bridge is above. Visit the abandoned village of Bastia or walk among the ancient chestnut trees of Valpiana and Val di Stornara.

→ About 15km NW of Santa Sofia (see previous swims) or from Forlì, take the SS67 towards San Benedetto in Alpe. After 38km you will reach Bocconi, a district of San Benedetto. At the restaurant La Beccona, turn L, following the signs for the car park and for the waterfall. Start walking; on the R there is a partially-cobbled path. To descend, turn L before the bridge and follow the edge of the field until you reach a small path.

10 mins easy, 44.0072, 11.7466

88 FIUME MONTONE

A Casa Cantonale

In this narrow stretch of the river, there are two pools almost 20 metres in diameter, framed by a small waterfall flowing over layers of rock. Other pools are located at both ends of the meander.

→ Continue on past Bocconi (swim 87) and after 2.5km (near the 150 kilometre post) you will pass the ruined pink house 'Casa Cantonale' on the R. 150m further and there is a bend to the R and a gap in the guard rail on the L (there's room for one car to park here on L). Descend on the rough path beneath the road embankment.

2 mins moderate, 43.9960, 11.7272

B The Briglia

This small pool at the foot of a bank is great for a quick stop.

→ About 2km after Casa Cantonale (see above), after a building entirely made of stone, park your car (148km post). From there, take the small path down to the river.

5 mins moderate, 43.9945, 11.7081

89 CASCATE DELL'ACQUACHETA

Many rivulets cascade down over layered sandstone, an impressive drop of about 70 metres. It's a lovely trail down to the falls, through the forests of the Parco Nazionale delle Foreste Casentinesi. The trail largely follows the course of the river. Immediately after the viewing belvedere you will come across the Lavane Waterfall, the best place to swim and cool off after the walk.

→ Continue on from Bocconi (above) to reach San Benedetto in Alpe. Bear R on the SP55 in the direction of Marradi, and after about 2km park in a layby near a bend where you will see an oak tree with very exposed roots. Walk up to the beginning of the path (footpath number CAI 415/A). At the first fork, bear R (CAI 407). Continue along the river, until you reach Mulino dei Romiti and stay on the uphill path (CAI 407). You will arrive at the next junction and see the belvedere viewing point for the waterfall. Continue straight on CAI 407 as far as the Lavane Waterfall (43.9923, 11.6449). Keep L and continue to I Romiti, then turn L. Cross the plateau and leave the path to follow the stream until you find the top of the waterfall.

120 mins easy, 43.9908, 11.6458

91A

Pietra di Bismantova

Head north to where the Fiume Santerno flows near Moraduccio. Here you can see the Cascata del Rio dei Briganti fall from a high cliff into a series of large pools surrounded by white rocks 90A. Above is the mysterious abandoned village of Castiglioncello, an eerie place to explore and wander.

A short way to the south-east, near Coniale, you can enjoy a fantastic picnic spot at the long pools of the Ponte di Camaggiore 90B. The stone bridge also leads to the old village of Camaggiore. However, there are many other places along the road where you can bathe and swim, most of them visible from the road (SP610).

Continue your journey north to the Secchia valley in Reggio Emilia province. The famous Bismantova rock rises out of the hazel forest, a steep-sided, table-topped limestone plateau that is a favourite among climbers and abseilers. There is a the man-made waterfall near the Fiume Secchia 91A and also Talada, where you can enjoy warm pools, and more picnic spots 91B. The highlight, however, is the Cascata Golfarone in the Val d'Asta to the west, hidden in the middle of the Parco Regionale dell'Alto Apennino Reggiano 92. There are great views, and a natural swimming pool with its own gentle whirlpool. To get to the falls, you must follow the course of the river, listening out for the waterfall in the distance.

▶

Glarola

Central Emilia Romagna - Santerno and Secchia rivers

90 FIUME SANTERNO

A Cascata del Rio dei Briganti

A tall plume of water falls over white rocks neatly layered in deep block slabs. There is a large, pleasant pool. This is an ideal place for a picnic and very easy to access. It is also well-known and can get busy, but in the evening it's quieter. You must visit the abandoned village of Castiglioncello, following the road after the bridge. A ghostly place.

→ Moraduccio lies along the SP610 in the direction of, but N of Firenzuola. Immediately SW of Moraduccio, turn W into a little road downhill, and park after the bridge in the car park. Cross and go down the path to the river.

1 min easy, 44.1754, 11.4855

B The Ponte di Camaggiore

Under this stone bridge there is a long pool, with several other pools nearby, all framed by the smooth slabs of rock, perfect for stretching out on comfortably. The stone bridge leads on to the old village of Camaggiore.

→ Continue SW along the SP610 from Moraduccio, past Coniale, until you reach a sharp R turning that leads down to a narrow bridge (signed Camaggiore). Cross over the bridge, and park just after in the laybys. Walk down to the river from here.

1 min easy, 44.1465, 11.4546

C The Mulino di Coniale

A long, deep river pool near a bend close to the old Coniale Mill, where there are also two small pebble beaches.

→ Coming from Moraduccio, 250m after the turning on the L for Tirli, and 700m before the Camaggiore bridge (above), bear R down a small unsigned road. Pass the houses, and continue over the bridge. Carry on until you can find an open space to leave your car. Just ahead, a lane leads down to the river.

1 min easy, 44.1530, 11.4534

91 FIUME SECCHIA, REGGIO EMILIA

A Giarola

This inviting jade pool lies below an old weir made of concrete and stone.

→ Travel over 60km to the NW. From the SS63 near Busana, take the SP18 towards Ligonchio. Continue on the SP18, through Marmoreto, and over the river bridge. Just before the next hairpin bend (50m), take the dirt road on the R, and park before the big house. Follow the road to the river.

3 mins easy, 44.3554, 10.3141

B Talada

Here the Fiume Secchia flows calmly over a broad bed, forming lovely pools. The water is warm and not very deep, and the beach is pebbled. A great spot for families to picnic surrounded by hills and nature.

→ From Busana, take the SS63 and turn R when you see the sign for Talada. Turn R in the village and take the road downhill, past the houses, through fields and woods. At the end of the road, leave your car and go down to the river.

3 mins easy, 44.3732, 10.3498

93

94A

North towards Parma, through the numerous valleys of the Apennines, you will pass through the Alta Valle del Taro, known for its wild mushrooms. Here people are attracted to the unspoilt, wild settings: pristine pools of emerald-green water, and great hiking. Near the tiny hamlet of Foppiano 95 you can relax in the clear pools of the Fiume Taro, surrounded by the beautiful landscape of beech and chestnut trees. There's also the Lido del Groppo 97, a small beach often crowded at weekends and in August, but with perfect rocks to dive from. There are several charming villages nearby which are good for exploring and buying local produce: Borgotaro makes a good base for mushroom hunters, Santa Maria del Taro is a pleasant mountain town and Castello di Bardi makes an interesting diversion.

End your trip north of Bedonia near Bobbio, on the Spiaggia Berlina 98A, where you can jump from upto 8 metres high. A few kilometres away, the small village of Brugnello 98C has the perfect view out to the Fiume Trebbia. Below the village, walk along the pebbly beach or relax in one of the pools, let the waters flow over you and soak up the beauty of this stunning region.

The Golfarone Falls and the Ansa dei Graniti

92 CASCATA GOLFARONE
In the middle of the Parco Regionale dell'Alto Appenino Reggiano, you'll find a huge, deep, blue rock pool, created by the Cascata Golfarone. To get there you must follow the course of the river between the smaller pools, guided by the distant sound of the falls. The waterfall spills from 15 metres high creating a wonderful jacuzzi whirlpool. You can swim or just sunbathe on the rocks.

➜ 10km NE of Busana on the SS63 (see swim 91 above) turn off R towards Villa Minozzo (SP19). Pass through the village and then Case Zobbi (1km). Continue on, through the hamlet Case Ferrari, and after about 3km, near a bend to the L after a bridge, you will see a small layby to park in (44.3220, 10.4614). Follow the path and it will take about 30 minutes to reach the river. Walk up-river for about 15 minutes, until you get to the waterfall, or stop along the way in the pool of your choice.

25 mins moderate, 44.3194, 10.4623

93 ANSA DEI GRANITI
The Ansa dei Graniti is a stretch of the Fiume Ceno, remarkable for the two huge granite monoliths perched on the bank of the river. These form the setting for these natural crystalline pools, surrounded by mountains. Going up the river, you can find some good places to camp. Cross the bridge and you will come to another deep pool surrounded by a high wall of granite.

➜ 40km NW from Cascate Golfarone (swim 92 above) and SW of Parma. Exit the A15 / E33 at Fornovo and take the SP28 towards Bardi (35km). When at Bardi, take the SP359 towards Bedonia. After the 66km post you will find a brown sign indicating a L turn to the Ansa dei Graniti. Turn and continue past the old mill. Park the car by the paddock fence. From here, walk along the path that goes towards the huge boulders ahead of you.

3 mins easy, 44.6217, 9.6939

94 ROCCAMURATA

A La Cava
Roccamurata is a quiet and secluded location where you'll find a lovely pool in the shade of a cliff. A little further upstream there's a second pool.

➜ Take the Borgotaro exit from the A15/E33, S of Palma. Follow the SP308 towards Roccamurata / Borgo Val di Taro. Go through Roccamurata and turn R before the tunnel, at a wide junction signed Gorro 3km. Continue straight (dead end) and on the R you will find a dirt road; leave your car here.

2 mins easy, 44.5279, 9.8622

B La Pietra
In the middle of this beautiful pool stands a large rock with a huge tree on top carried there by the river; a reminder of the river's strength.

➜ Entering Roccamurata, as above, and just before the turning L into the village, turn sharp R down to the bridge. Turn R again after the bridge and park after 400m.

2 mins easy, 44.5372, 9.8828

95A

95B

95B

97

Upper Taro Valley

95 FOPPIANO, FIUME TARO

The Alta Valle del Taro offers spectacular views with green pools of clear water among forests of beech and chestnut. It's a pleasant place to pause after visiting the many beautiful villages on the slopes of the Apennines. The area is also famous for its delicious wild mushrooms that can be collected in the woods (with a permit).

A Upstream

A stunning natural pool with a striking sandstone rock rising out of the waters. Ideal for diving or stopping to sunbathe. You will also find two small pebble beaches where you can lay out your towels.

→ From Borgo Val de Taro (see previous swims) continue W on the SP4 to Bedonia. Take the SP359 (direction Santa Maria del Taro) 9 km until the turning to Foppiano. 200m beyond you will find a yellow house on the R. Park on the other side of the road and look for the path that leads down to the river, on the R side of the house.

2 mins easy, 44.4664, 9.5799

B Downstream

Close to a ford the Fiume Taro forms a large, deep pool, perfect for swimming. Crossing the river you can easily find places to camp in the woods. Downstream there is another pool, narrow but longer than the previous one, and with a high rock.

→ Head back towards Bedonia 1.5km on the SP359 (see above), and 500m before the sandstone processing company on your L, park on the outside of a R bend, in a layby. From there, take the dirt track down to the river.

1 min easy, 44.4757, 9.5892

96 PIANE DI CARNIGLIA, FIUME TARO

Near two weirs on the river there are several pools, quite easy to reach. Not the most romantic place in the valley, but it's pleasant enough for a refreshing dip. Downstream after the bridge, depending on the river flow, a small island makes a good place to camp. Between Piane di Carniglia and Foppiano, there are many pools just waiting to be discovered.

→ Continue back along the SP359, 5km before Bedonia; before Piane di Carniglia you will find a large parking area just before the bridge, near the wooden board. You will immediately see the first pool. Up the river there are two more pools.

1 min easy, 44.4812, 9.6091

97 LIDO DEL GROPPO, FIUME TARO

Nestled in a meander on the Fiume Taro, Lido del Groppo is an attractive beach with a small shop, overlooking a deep lake. There is a perfect rock for diving. It can get very crowded in August and on weekends.

→ Continue on towards Bedonia on SP359 and just as you are entering the outskirts, turn R for Tornolo (SP24). After the bridge turn L, park, and go down to the river.

1 min easy, 44.4917, 9.6321

98A Spiaggia Berlina

98B

98B

98A

Brugnello

98 FIUME TREBBIA

The Fiume Trebbia, with its crystal-clear waters, wide streams and narrow loops, offers a number of options for those seeking places to swim and dive.

A Spiaggia Berlina

Shortly after Bobbio, in Berlina, there is a beach frequently used by the locals. Here the river forms two broad lakes. The one upstream is quite deep, and the high cliffs on the sides mean you can jump in from different heights of up to 8 metres. The pool downstream is bordered by a wide beach of large pebbles. There is also a campsite nearby.

➔ Bobbio is on the SS45, 40km NW of Bedonia (previous swims). Head S out of Bobbio on the SS45 in the direction of Marsaglia. Turn L after about 1km, before the campsite and the main river bridge, and follow the signs for Coli. After the bridge turn R, and R again at the first crossroads. Follow the road until you get to a car park. Park and walk along the visible path. The second pool is about 50m upstream from the first. You can stay over at Camping Pontegobbo on the river banks △ (Tel. 0523 936927).
2 mins easy, 44.7491, 9.3790

B Perino

Along the SS45 road there are a number of easy-to-reach pools. The water is not too deep and the current is calm. Walking up the river a little from where you have parked the car, you will see a large boulder, looming over a lovely pool where small waterfalls form a natural jacuzzi.

➔ 12km N of Bobbio on the SS45, just before the village of Perino, turn L following the signs for Donceto. Immediately after the bridge turn L and take the dirt road that continues straight ahead. Park at the end, and on your L you will find paths going down to the river.
2 mins easy, 44.8196, 9.4832

C Brugnello

Just below the picturesque village of Brugnello, the Fiume Trebbia takes tortuous route forced by narrow bends into a series of beautiful pools surrounded by large pebbly beaches.

➔ From Bobbio follow the SS45 S again in the direction of Marsaglia. The road follows the river until you reach a very twisty stretch where the Trebbia forms large loops. After the second bend, about 7km from Bobbio, you will find a wide turning to the L. Park just before that where there are spaces. Look for the dirt path that will take you to the river. The beach is pebbly and it's fun to explore the small pools that have formed. Follow the river until you find your favourite one.
2 mins easy, 44.7202, 9.3910

107A Lago di Vico, the beach of Santa Lucia

Lazio & Umbria

Just a few miles from Rome you will find volcanic crater lakes, dark sand beaches and one of the biggest waterfalls in the world.

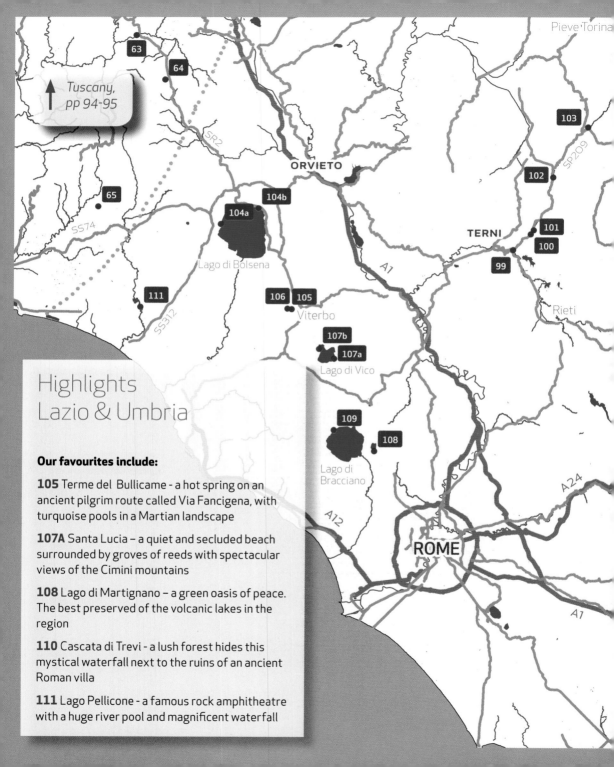

Tuscany,
pp 94-95

63

64

65

103

102

ORVIETO

SR2

SS74

104b

104a

TERNI

101

100

99

Lago di Bolsena

111

A1

SS312

106 **105**

Viterbo

Rieti

107b

107a

Lago di Vico

Highlights
Lazio & Umbria

109

108

Our favourites include:

Lago di
Bracciano

A24

105 Terme del Bullicame - a hot spring on an
ancient pilgrim route called Via Fancigena, with
turquoise pools in a Martian landscape

A12

107A Santa Lucia – a quiet and secluded beach
surrounded by groves of reeds with spectacular
views of the Cimini mountains

ROME

108 Lago di Martignano – a green oasis of peace.
The best preserved of the volcanic lakes in the
region

110 Cascata di Trevi - a lush forest hides this
mystical waterfall next to the ruins of an ancient
Roman villa

A1

111 Lago Pellicone - a famous rock amphitheatre
with a huge river pool and magnificent waterfall

Pieve Torina

SP209

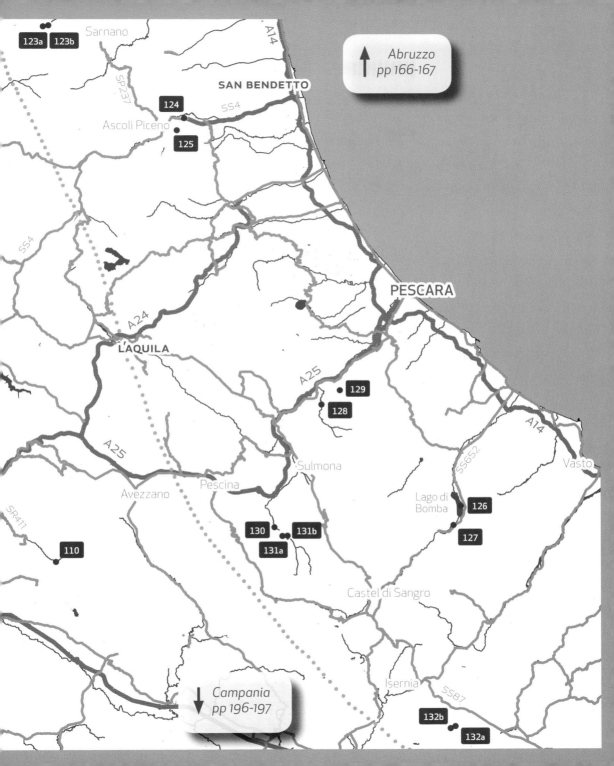

Abruzzo
pp 166-167

123a 123b

Sarnano

124

SAN BENDETTO

SP237

SS4

Ascoli Piceno

125

SS4

A14

A24

L'AQUILA

A25

PESCARA

129

128

A25

A14

SS652

Vasto

Sulmona

Pescina

Avezzano

Lago di
Bomba

126

127

SR411

110

130

131b

131a

Castel di Sangro

Campania
pp 196-197

Isernia

SS87

132b

132a

99

Basilica of Assisi

Generally when people visit this region it's to immerse themselves in its history and art. Rome, 'the eternal city', is the perfect example; visiting Rome would be enough on its own to fill one trip, but other small towns like Ostia Antica, Todi, Perugia and Assisi could also keep you busy for a lifetime. So if you prefer to escape the tourists, and hustle and bustle of the city, do as the Romans do and retreat to the green hills and volcanic lakes of Lazio or visit the charming and colourful hills of Umbria, with hot springs and majestic waterfalls.

We recommend you start north of Rome in Perugia, the capital city of Umbria, in the mountainous area of south-east Umbria. After a walk around the beautiful and historic centre, enjoying the fresh air of this university town, head south on the SS75 towards the Valnerina, the narrow and winding Apennine valley of the Fiume Nera, to Terni. Here you will find many ancient villages and ▶

101. Arrone

The Valnerina, southern Umbria

99 CASCATA DELLE MARMORE

The highest waterfall in Italy and the highest man-made waterfall in the world. Go to the upper panoramic viewpoint path as it gives spectacular views to the various levels of this gigantic waterfall. Go to the lower path and you will be very close to it and its power although, for safety reasons, it is forbidden to swim.

→ For the lower view point: from the SS675/E45 exit at Terni Est and from there follow the signs for Valnerina/Cascata delle Marmore. Take the SS3, then the SR209. The car park is on this road on the R. For the upper view point: take Terni Est exit then SS79 towards Rieti, to Marmore, following signs for 'Cascata'. The B&B 'La Porta della Valnerina' (Tel 347 7609678) is a great place to stay near a beautiful stretch of the river, with natural pools and small caves.

30 mins easy, 42.5529, 12.7149

100 CENTRO RAFTING, MARMORE

At Marmore's rafting centre, upstream of the falls, there's a grassy beach with picnic tables nearby. The water is not deep but

the current is fast and it's fun to ride the flow (keep an eye on the children though!) Here you can enjoy activities such as white water-rafting under the Marmore waterfall, canoeing and hydrospeed (also known as riverboarding).

→ From the waterfall (above) continue along the SR209 towards Fontechiaruccia, 6km from the lower waterfall car park, then turn R at the roundabout (with a sculpture in the middle) towards Arrone. Cross the bridge and after 100m turn very sharp L at the pedestrian crossing, down to the river. The car park for the rafting centre is ahead 🏖.
1 min easy, 42.5875, 12.7661

101 ARRONE, FIUME NERA

A little river beach on the Fiume Nera, just upstream from Arrone. The water is deep and you can swim in the stream near a small grassy beach. There are plenty of trees for shade during the hottest hours of the day, and the surrounding landscape is quiet and pleasant.

→ Head to the rafting centre car park (see above) and then head down the small side street on the R, with houses on both sides.

Park along the road and continue walking until you come to the beach on your L.
1 min easy, 42.5917, 12.7715

102 SCHEGGINO, FIUME NERA

A quiet beach under a neat row of trees. The water is not deep and the grassy area is ideal for a picnic with children.

→ Continue N on the SR209 about 15km to reach Scheggino. At the village, turn R into the car park before the bridge. The beach is just downstream.
1 min easy, 42.7139, 12.8307

103 TRIPONZO, FIUME NERA

Two small, shallow hidden pools next to a small beach. The current here is moderate (keep an eye on the kids) but also fun.

→ Continue N on the SR209 another 10km to Borgo Cerreto. Keep going on SR209 (in the direction of Visso) and 200m after the SR320 junction you will see a small dirt road that descends to the R. Park here and follow to the river.
5 mins easy, 42.8252, 12.9308

99 Cascata delle Marmore

104A

104A

the Cascata delle Marmore **99**, the highest waterfall in Italy and the highest artificial waterfall in the world, reaching 165 metres with three spectacular stages. Unfortunately, because it powers hydroelectric plants, the flow of the waterfall varies throughout the year; however, it's amazing to observe the force of the water crashing towards the bottom. It's also a great river-rafting location, provided by the Centro Rafting Marmore **100**, which also has a pleasant place to paddle and swim.

Head upstream, along the SR209, to the town of Scheggino **102**, where there's a little beach with shallow pools; a great place for the kids; and further on towards Visso **103** where there's another spot with a small beach and little pools to explore. The current here is quite strong, so be careful with the little ones.

Next head east, roughly 140 kilometres, to the city of Orvieto, where you can enjoy a beautiful sunset. The city, perched on top of a flat volcanic rock, overlooks the valley of the river Paglia offering breathtaking panoramas. We recommend you take a look at the brilliant architecture of the grand 14th century Roman Catholic cathedral while you're there. From here, the hills of northern Lazio welcome you as you travel towards the Lago di Bolsena **104** (35 kilometres west of Orvieto). This volcanic crater lake is nestled in a pleasant landscape of woods, olive groves, vineyards and fields, ▶

104

104 LAGO DI BOLSENA

A volcanic crater lake surrounded by gentle hills where time passes slowly. The waters are the cleanest among European lakes, its climate is mild and its beaches are composed of dark volcanic sand. The western shore is wild and the eastern shore is dotted with small towns. In the south you will find large fields separated from the water by narrow beaches.

A West shore

This quiet shore is separated from the traffic by an olive grove, creating a quiet and relaxing atmosphere.

→ The lake is easily accessible and well-signposted from Pitigliano, Orvieto and Viterbo. From Bolsena, head W on the SR2, bearing L on SS489 towards Gradoli. Before Gradoli turn L to Capodimonte and after 5km bear L towards the shore. Once at the end of the road, near the wooden sign, park and follow the pedestrian path.
2 mins easy, 42.6094, 11.8672

B Bolsena beach

After visiting the lovely town of Bolsena cool off in the quiet and secluded beach located at the north-western edge of the village. This is the quietest of the often busy beaches along this stretch.

→ In the village, head down Via Cristoforo Colombo the near Hotel Nazionale. At the end of the street, turn R and continue until the road becomes pedestrian. You will see the car park and the lake from here. The restaurant 🍴 La Pineta (Tel 0761 799 801) cooks dishes with fish from the lake. There are many campsites located along the lake, such as the four star ⛺ Lido Camping Village (Tel 0761 799 258).
2 mins easy, 42.6444, 11.9754

105 TERME DEL BULLICAME

This hot spring flows out from an underground crater at 58C and feeds two pools through channels carved into the rock. The smallest pool has a very high temperature, but the larger pool is much cooler. Bring plenty of water to drink, plus all the essentials as there are

no facilities around. The Terme is closed at night.

→ From Bolsena head S on the SR2 to Viterbo, then S on the SS675. Exit at Viterbo Centro, turn L and L again onto Strada del Bullicame, heading W. 200m after the motorway bridge, turn R onto a dirt road following along the botanical garden fence. You will have to park on the side of the road. Turn back and the path for the baths is on the R.
1 min easy, 42.4207, 12.0741

106 PISCINE CARLETTI, VITERBO

Two small and two large rectangular pools, all connected to each other. The water here reaches 58C and there are no shady areas or facilities, but it is open in the evenings.

→ From the Terme del Bullicame carry along Strada del Bullicame, turn R onto SP15, then turn L and after 300m. Park on the side of the road.
1 min easy, 42.4217, 12.0646

106

105

107B

108

and is surrounded by dark-coloured sand. The west coast 104A is wild and there are plenty of beaches to enjoy. The east coast is more populated, but has a nice secluded beach on the edge of the pretty village of Bolsena 104B.

Next head towards the ancient city of Viterbo (south on SR2) in the region of Lazio. Just outside the city to the west are the Terme del Bullicame 105, mentioned by Dante in The Divine Comedy. These are free thermal baths and the water comes from a small crater now protected by a fence. It's about 58C in temperature and it flows through a series of small channels to feed into a pair of turquoise pools. There are no facilities of any kind, so remember to bring some drinking water with you, and perhaps a sun umbrella and some sun cream, as the few fig trees around the pools don't create much shade on a hot summer's day.

After a warming soak in the hot thermal pools, a visit to swim in Lago di Vico (south on SP1), surrounded by the Cimini mountains, will seem like a dream. According to legend, this lake depression was created by the club of Hercules as a sign of defiance towards the inhabitants of the area. Actually it is volcanic in origin. You will find many beaches here, such as the small and secluded Località Santa Lucia 107A and, on the north-side of the lake, the half-moon-shaped Fondo Cencio 107B, situated at the edge of the forest. ▶

Vico and Martignano Lakes, Western Lazio

107 LAGO DI VICO

A small crater lake and nature reserve with views of the Cimini Mountains. It is warm and you can soak quietly in the clear water; however you may find the bottom slightly muddy. The lake shore is often reedy.

A Santa Lucia

A small, secluded beach sheltered by trees and tall reeds. On your way you will pass beautiful hazel woods.

➜ From Viterbo (see previous swim) head S on the SP1 for 20km. 900m after restaurant 'Due Cigni' turn R, opposite the petrol station, and following signs to the nature reserve 'Lago di Vico'. At the end of the road turn R, carry on 300m until you get to the church, and turn L onto the dirt road opposite. Not far away there is the brilliant campsite, Camping Natura ▲, famous for its ecological support (Tel. 0761 612347). Kayaks 🛶 are also available to rent on the beach.

1 min easy, 42.3096, 12.1979

B Fondo Cencio

A half-moon shaped beach at the edge of the forest, with grass, reeds and small bushes that you can shelter under and hide within. Wild and hidden.

➜ Continue along the SP1 upto the junction with the SP39 and turn R, in the direction of S.Martino al Cimino. 6km after Punta del Lago, you will find a car park on the L of a large picnic area. Walk along the shore of the lake heading N.

3 mins easy, 42.3314, 12.1538

108 LAGO DI MARTIGNANO

This small lake is located in a green valley managed as a nature reserve with limited access by car. It is busy on summer weekends, but during the week it is an little oasis of peace. The water is clean and there are green meadows and trees that you can nap under. Most of the area is public access, but there are also some private beaches where you can rent beach chairs, paddle boats and canoes. Nearby you can also enjoy beautiful walks around the lush lakeside.

➜ About 10km S of Lago di Vico (above). The roads leading to Lago di Martignano are part of a restricted traffic area, so it may not be possible to arrive by car. In the summer you should inquire locally. If you do drive, from Anguillara you can take Via della Mola Vecchia and after about 1.5km turn L into Via Comunale di Cesano. From here walk up to a large car park. During periods when access to this road is limited, there is a shuttle service leaving from a car park in Via della Mola Vecchia in Anguillara (42.0896, 12.2935). Some local companies will provide their guests passes that allow them to reach the lake, even during periods when there is a restriction. The organic farm Agriturismo Il Castoro ▲ (Tel. 0699 80202) has space for tents, and has an excellent 🍴 restaurant.

30 mins easy, 42.1042, 12.3161

110

111

111 Rainbow Bridge

If you're after some small luxuries, also on the SP1 is the small Lago di Martignano 108, a good choice for your next swim. You will find it located in the south of the Parco Naturale Regionale di Bracciano-Martignano. Here you can rent beach chairs, canoes and paddle boats. Set deep in the countryside it also has some good walks in the surrounding woods.

Head only 20 kilometres north on the SP11 and you'll find the Lago Bracciano 109, the second largest lake in this region. The beautiful environment is sometimes disturbed by the crowds, but don't let that spoil your trip as there are many hidden spots to discover as well.

We finish the tour in the valley of the Parco Naturale Monti Simbruini, on the Fiume Aniene (south-east from Lake Bracciano) where the Cascata di Trevi 110 provides a relaxing pool, luscious greenery and places to pitch a tent, perfect for rejuvenating before the next journey.

Lago del Pellicone

Western and Eastern Lazio

109 LAGO BRACCIANO, NORTH-WEST

A popular destination on the weekend for many Romans, this lake is often crowded and noisy, but it is located in a beautiful and natural setting. Fortunately motor boats are prohibited, and once in the water you can find a bit of peace.

→ From Anguillara (see previous swim) take the SP11b then SP1f lake shore road W to and through Bracciano. Continue along the lake and eventually you will find several laybys with paths leading to the beaches.

1 min easy, 42.1509, 12.1979

110 CASCATA DI TREVI

A wonderful waterfall hidden in a lush, dense forest, with a beautiful pool to swim below. The suns seeps in, it radiates a mystical atmosphere to the whole area. Nearby there are also the ruins of an ancient Roman villa and aqueduct. A little further upstream, along the road that leads to the waterfall, you could pitch your tent on

the banks of the river near the small blue pools.

→ From Frosinone (A1/E45, SE of Rome) follow the SS155 20km N, via Alatri. Bear R onto the SR411 towards Altipiani di Arcinazzo. After the town, turn R onto the SP28 towards Trevi nel Lazio. Follow this road for about 5km, then turn L near a shrine, towards Jenne. Carry on other 4km, and near a bridge you will find a kiosk and a restaurant. Go over the bridge and on the R you will see the parking spaces with the path that leads to the waterfall.

5 mins easy, 41.8664, 13.1937

111 LAGO DEL PELLICONE

In the middle of the Parco di Vulci, in Northern Lazio, the Fiume Flora forms a very picturesque large pool, surrounded by high volcanic cliffs, where a waterfall falls between the towering rocks. The water is usually clear, but on occasion it can be muddy. You can dive from the rocks and from some trees that have ropes. You can visit the Parco di Vulci on foot or head to the Castello di Vulci to

see the stunning Ponte dell'Arcobaleno, (Rainbow Bridge) spanning the gorge of the Fiume Flora.

→ From Montalto di Castro, drive along the SS312 in the direction of Lago di Bolsena. After about 5km ,turn L towards Vulci (SP106). After 5km arrive at the junction with the SP107 and turn L (Parco di Vulci). Continue to the castello and cross the bridge over the Fiume Flora, and then turn L into the park. At the visitor centre you can leave your car. (If you arrive early you can walk in for free; otherwise you will have to pay admission to the park.) Walk along the white road you were driving along, and then turn L onto the road downhill. Follow the trees to the woods and continue to follow the road, to arrive at the huge river pool.

15 mins easy, 42.4251, 11.6351

Cascata di Trevi

Abruzzo, Molise & Le Marche

Enjoy turquoise gorges, picturesque lakes and green rockpools, from the wild Apennine valleys to the gentle hills that fade into the sea.

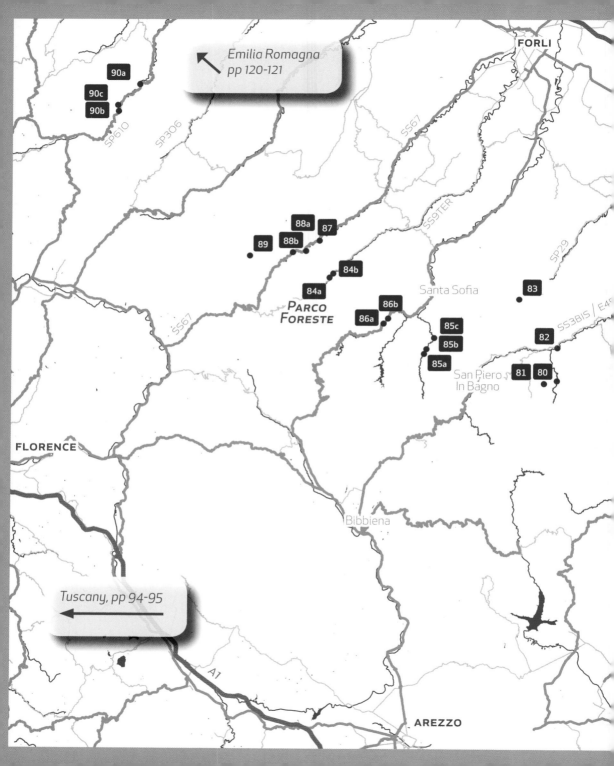

FORLI

Emilia Romagna
pp 120-121

90a

90c

90b

SP610

SP306

SS67

SS9TER

SP29

88a

87

89

88b

84b

84a

Santa Sofia

83

PARCO
FORESTE

86b

86a

85c

SS3BIS / E45

82

85b

85a

81   80

San Piero
In Bagno

FLORENCE

Tuscany, pp 94-95

Bibbiena

A1

AREZZO

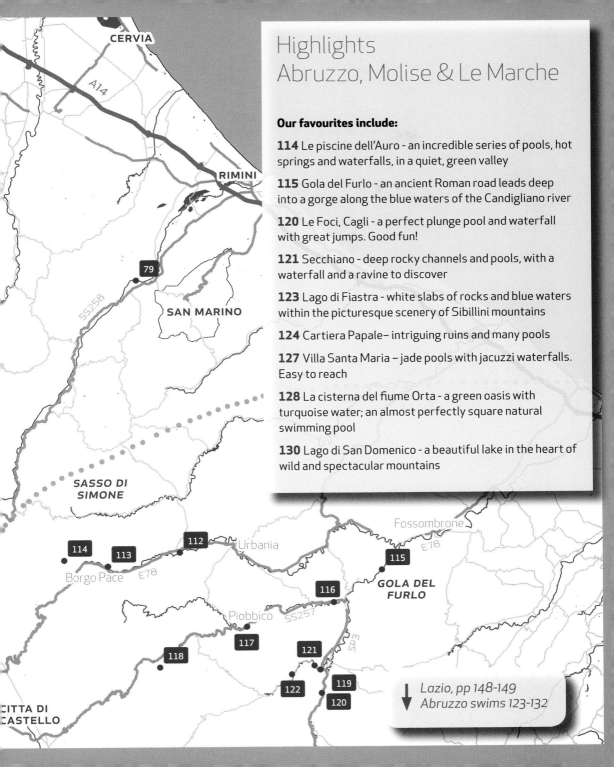

Highlights
Abruzzo, Molise & Le Marche

Our favourites include:

114 Le piscine dell'Auro - an incredible series of pools, hot springs and waterfalls, in a quiet, green valley

115 Gola del Furlo - an ancient Roman road leads deep into a gorge along the blue waters of the Candigliano river

120 Le Foci, Cagli - a perfect plunge pool and waterfall with great jumps. Good fun!

121 Secchiano - deep rocky channels and pools, with a waterfall and a ravine to discover

123 Lago di Fiastra - white slabs of rocks and blue waters within the picturesque scenery of Sibillini mountains

124 Cartiera Papale– intriguing ruins and many pools

127 Villa Santa Maria – jade pools with jacuzzi waterfalls. Easy to reach

128 La cisterna del fiume Orta - a green oasis with turquoise water; an almost perfectly square natural swimming pool

130 Lago di San Domenico - a beautiful lake in the heart of wild and spectacular mountains

Lazio, pp 148-149
Abruzzo swims 123-132

114 Le Piscine dell'Auro

114

The true nature of the Marche and Abruzzo mountains remains hidden from the passing tourist, and their alluring, picturesque valleys and villages are best discovered slowly. The landscapes and colours always have one more revelation in store, from the peaks of the Apennines down to the narrow coastal plain.

The Marche region is full of little surprises. Begin your journey by visiting the Cascata del Sasso, on the Metauro river. This waterfall is one of the ten largest in Italy and is a favourite spot for fishermen too **112**. Just 10 minutes upstream to the west, on the edge of the small medieval village of Mercatello sul Metauro, you will find beautiful small waterfalls and two pools to swim in. This is a great area for a picnic or barbecue, and there are facilities provided in the park nearby **113**.

▶

114

Metauro Valley

112 CASCATA DEL SASSO

A large waterfall that falls from a rock wall into a deep pool. It is the biggest on the River Metauro, about 60m long and 12m high. The only bad point is that it's situated near a noisy industrial area.

➜ From Sant'Angelo in Vado, exit the E78 near the industrial area where you will find the sign 'Cascata del Sasso' on via Cà Maspino. Go to the end of the street and turn L, until you reach a small gravel/grass car park. A little further on there is a path R leading to the river.

1 mins easy, 43.6678, 12.4350

113 MERCATELLO SUL METAURO

A stunning river that bends under a high cliff. You will find small waterfalls and two pools, among flaked rocks that seem to fall apart in the sun. Perfect for picnics with the family, as large trees and small clefts in the rock provide shade during the hottest hours. Nearby there is a pleasant park with tables and a barbecue.

➜ From Sant'Angelo in Vado, take the E78 to Mercatello sul Metauro. In the village turn R onto Via IV Novembre. Take 2nd L onto Via Campo Sportivo and pass the sportfield to find parking on right. From here go up the river a little to get to the lakes and waterfalls.

3 mins easy, 43.6532, 12.3309

114 LE PISCINE DELL'AURO

The Auro valley has a magnificent series of easily accessible waterfalls and natural pools. The river flows over large rock steps, which lead down toward the union with the Meta river. The valley is sparsely populated but is full of lush greenery. There are pools to suit all, from the beautiful but dangerous Gorga dei Morti, to the quiet Poderina where there is also a sulphur spring, and the pretty Madonnina and Obbra pools. Our advice is to try them all.

➜ From Mercatello sul Metauro continue on the E78 in the direction of Borgo Pace. At the town, turn R onto the SP61. Once through and out of the town, keep L following the signs for Parchiule. After 1km, turn R at a small wooden sign that signals the natural swimming pool 'I Morti'. Park and go down to the river. Along this road that leads from Borgo Pace to Parchiule you will also find signs for the pool 'La Madonnina' (43.6577, 12.2589).

1 mins moderate, 43.6598, 12.2673

113

113

113

117 Fosso dell'Eremo

118

115

West from Mercatello sul Metauro, towards the Valle dell'Auro, the plain begins to narrow and the woodland grows wilder. You will find a great number of natural swimming pools here such as the Piscine dell'Auro, near the town of Borgo Pace **114**.

If you head east you come to the town of Urbania, which has been a centre of ceramics since the 15th century, and then on to the Palazzo Ducale in the walled city of Urbino. The palace is an architectural gem and the cradle of the Renaissance, which is reflected throughout the entire city.

South-east from Urbino is the spectacular Gola del Furlo, a Natural Reserve that is home to a range of rare flora and fauna. The tranquil waters of the river Candigliano flow beside a narrow Roman road, making a charming drive. The first tunnel was dug in 76AD and has a path which for millennia has been used to cross the steep walls of the mountains of Pietralata and Paganuccio **115**. Once out of the gorge, forests and mountains give way to fertile valleys. At Acqualagna take some time to visit the Roman Abbey of San Vincenzo, one of the oldest Benedictine monasteries in the Marche region.

▶

115 Gola del Furlo

River Candigliano

115 GOLA DEL FURLO
A deep gorge where the turquoise waters of the quiet Candigliano form a beautiful lake. You will find it is spectacular to walk along the ancient Roman road overlooking the river, and also through the 76AD tunnel. Upstream from the gorge, a large well-shaded picnic area gives access to the river. Parco le Querce nearby has a lawned area to pitch your tent in. Friendly owners.

➜ From Acqualagna head N on local Via Flaminia – not SP3/Via Flaminia Nord! This becomes Strada Pianacce, then Via Monte Furlo, then Via Sant'Anna del Furlo. Furlo Gorge is on the right. Park your car where the road runs close to the water and walk to the lake.

1 mins easy, 43.6482, 12.7275

116 ACQUALAGNA
Wonderful rocky beach in the middle of the village with narrow and elongated lakes, boulders from which to dive and trees with ropes to swing and jump into the water. Go down along the bank of the river and you will find other attractive pools and beaches.

➜ From Acqualagna take the SS257 up to a roundabout (on your R will be a large supermarket and on your L a truffles company). Take the second exit and then turn, coming to a small car park. Leave your car and take the dirt road R that leads to a little white building at the edge of a grove. Turn L here and you will arrive at the river.

2 min easy, 43.6132, 12.6575

117 FOSSO DELL'EREMO
A pool big enough to swim in, framed by a pebbly beach, and a river beautifully broken up into thousands of tiny bubbly channels by the rocks that make up its bed. After a relaxing picnic, move 200m further downstream and find waterfalls and canyons - perfect for swimming.

➜ From Acqualagna, take the SS257 towards Piobbico. About 14km from Acqualagna, before Piobbico, you will find a yellow sign on the left, before a bridge, stating 'Fosso dell'Eremo'. Park your car on the gravel car park on the R, and walk down to the river.

1 min easy, 43.5871, 12.5316

118 GORGACCIA
A small pool with a beautiful waterfall, completely immersed in a natural environment. It can be reached by a pleasant walk through woods and fields, crossing several times over a small stream. Beware of the small river crabs that hide among the stones.

➜ From Piobbico continue to Apecchio on strada Statale Appecchiese. 1km after exiting Appechio, look out on the L for a house, and take the turning next to it. Follow the signs for the Agriturismo Pieve San Paolo. Continue onto a pitch near the entrance of the house where you can park. From there follow the path that leads to the well-signed Gorgaccia.
🍴 Agriturismo Pieve San Paolo is great to stop and eat at. (Tel 0331 681 6056).

25 mins easy, 43.5434, 12.4054

116

116

116 Acqualagna

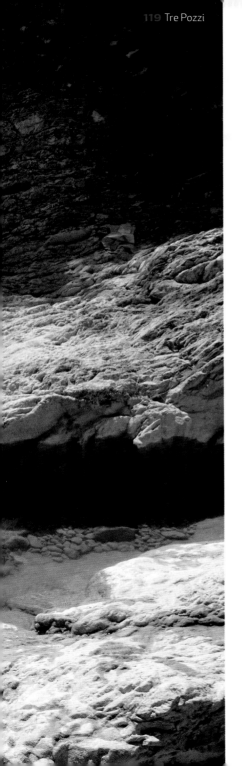

120

120

120

The rocky beach in the village of Acqualagna itself is perfect for families, as there are plenty of trees ropes to swing on and boulders to dive off 116. West from here is the Fosso dell'Eremo, another beautiful place for a picnic and a swim 117. Further south-west enjoy a pleasant walk through the woods to the waterfall and pool of Gorgaccia 118.

A little further south, the Bosso and Burano rivers create some of the most beautiful natural pools in the region. Tre Pozzi is a popular place as people like to dive near the old mill 119. Towards the north-east is Le Foci, near Cagli, with many waterfalls and little rock pools to explore 120. Carrying on north-east you will end up downstream of the river near Secchiano, where there are rock canyons surrounded by forest: great for hiking 121. Upstream of Secchiano there are sheltered quiet pools. Lie on the rocks and heat up, then dive in to cool down again 122.

Continue to head south and east to visit the vast and spectacular Grotte di Frasassi in Genga, full of stalactites and stalagmites. Afterwards drive on towards the magnificent Parco Nazionale dei Monti Sibillini: among the gorges, forests, grasslands and beautiful valleys here, you reach the very heart of the Apennines. ▶

Le Foci - Cagli

The Bosso and Burano rivers

119 TRE POZZI

Three Wells. An extraordinary stretch of stream, and a small gorge where it is popular to dive near an old mill. Fun and picturesque.

→ From Acqualagna, take the SP3 S and exit at Cagli Ovest. Turn R onto SP29, signposted Secchiano, and stop after 250m, just past a pink house, at the sign indicating you are leaving Cagli. There is a path that leads to the stream, and you will find many trails that guide you on to various pools. Take your time to explore the area.

2 mins easy, 43.5400, 12.6373

120 LE FOCI - CAGLI

A large swimming pool among the rocks where you can dive. Going up the river, a series of waterfalls and pools carved into the rock are fun to explore, with places to dive and water slides. There are also plenty of large rocks to sunbathe on.

→ From Tre Pozzi take the SP29 the short distance back to the SP3, turning

onto the sliproad signposted Roma. Exit at Gola del Burano, just after the tunnel, turn R signposted Foci (the opposite way from the more legible 'Ponte Romano' sign) and after 500m you will arrive. The pool can be seen from the road.

1 mins easy, 43.5150, 12.6390

121 DOWNSTREAM OF SECCHIANO

Here you will find steep canyons that enclose several pools. Beautiful rock formations frame the green of the forest, and upriver there are lakes between deep rocky channels. This is a great location to take a hike over, exploring each and every corner.

→ From Tre Pozzi, continue along SP29 towards Secchiano for about 1.5km, and you will find your destination on your right. Stop and take the path down to the river on the R at the first parking area next to the road. From the top of the hill you can overlook the river and choose your preferred spot. Other long and narrow lakes are reachable from parking opposite the

little white roadside church of Madonna del Cerbino (43.5411, 12.6319), which you will find about halfway between Tre Pozzi and here.

10 mins moderate, 43.5445, 12.6288

122 UPSTREAM OF SECCHIANO

This section of the river offers quiet pools of different sizes, some a few metres deep, others just a few centimetres. With both sunny rocks and shaded areas, this location is also ideal for families to have a picnic.

→ Continue to Secchiano, then follow SP29 south for 4km, to a large gravelled area on the L hand-side of the road. Park and follow the path down to the river. You will find the deeper pools are downstream of this point.

3 mins easy, 43.5350, 12.5963

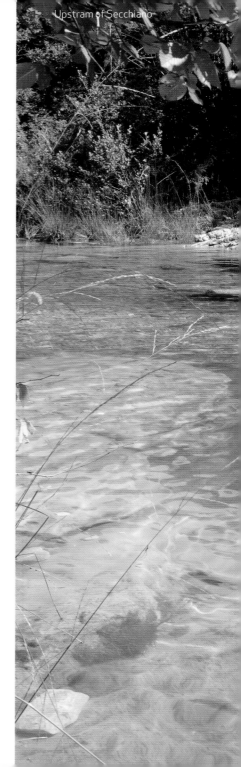

124

125

125

124

In this park, Lago di Fiastra is a perfect stop – a cool haven with white chalk beaches and white cliffs, surrounded by lush green grass and trees **123**, a superb backdrop to any holiday. The south shore has a long sandy beach to stroll along, with a great path for cyclists **123A**, and the north shore is excellent for camping, awakening to the sight of the cool water in the distance **123B**.

The Torrente Castellano near Ascoli Piceno is hidden among the beautiful vegetation with many little pools separated by gurgling waterfalls. Do not miss the Cartiera Papale, Paper mill of the Pope; full of natural pools and waterfalls **124**, nor the small but charming village of Castel Trosino, just 10 minutes south, with its wonderful views and relaxing pools and springs. One of these is L'Acqua Salmacina, a wonderful spring which flows into the river Castellano **125**.

Heading south, you pass into Abruzzo: gentle hills a short distance from the sea, surrounded by vineyards and olive groves, near the village of Pollutri. From there, head into the valley of the Sangro in Chieti, until you get to the long expanse of Lago di Bomba, in a beautiful landscape with places to stop for swimming, surfing, canoeing and many more outdoor activities **126**.

124 Cartiera Papale

Lake Fiastra and River Castellano

123 LAGO DI FIASTRA

A beautiful blue lake (in fact a reservoir) in the Sibillini mountains. With sandy beaches and stunning white rock tiers, it is easy to find a secluded spot to relax or, for more services, choose one of the popular beaches on the south. From the dam, have a beautiful trek to the Lame Rosse (Red Blades), rock formations that could be straight out of an old Western.

A South shore

A long sandy beach surrounded by a steep meadow. The pedestrian/cycle path along the shore makes a perfect walk for families.

→ From the medieval university town of Camerino, take SP132 heading S. After about 7km take the R onto Località Sfercia. Continue S on SS77. Turn L onto SP98. After crossing the dam you will find the first set of beaches in San Lorenzo al Lago. For more natural beaches continue on the SP91 for about 1.5km, park and take one of the trails to go down to the shore.

4 mins easy, 43.0528, 13.1752

B North shore

Beautiful beach with white slabs of rock and extremely clear water.

→ Return from the Sponda Meridionale along the SP91. When you reach San Lorenzo al Lago, turn R at the church, then L around it to cross the dam (great views here). At the first hairpin take the turning signposted Fiegni. After about 1.5km leave your in the gravel car park on the R. From here you will find the trail to the beach. Not far is the ◭ campsite Belvedere La Ruffella, for tents only, situated on a picturesque rocky headland (Tel 0737 527013).

4 mins easy, 43.0505, 13.1690

124 CARTIERA PAPALE

A wonderful collection of natural pools, beaches and waterfalls, with an easy access path. The water is always clear; dive in and the dense greenery will shelter you from the sun.

→ From the A14 exit at Porto d'Ascoli, join the motorway (S4) at Ascoli-Mare towards Ascoli Piceno. Take the 'Ascoli Piceno, Porta Cartara' exit, and follow signs for the centre. At the mini-roundabout take the first exit and then slight R fork after bridge onto Via della Cartiera. Park at end, cross the bridge and follow the path.

5 mins easy, 42.8489, 13.5690

125 L'ACQUA SALMACINA

Just below the wonderful village of Castel Trosino is a small spring which flows into the river Castellano, where you will find a small pool. Further up the river there are a couple of larger pools.

→ From the Cartiera dei Papi, go back to the mini-roundabout, take the first exit and carry on for approximately 4km to Casette. Near the start of Casette, you will see a sign for 'area archeologico ambientale, Lago di Casette' on a stone house on your R. Turn R and follow the road through Casette and past the hamlet 'Il Lago'. Cross the bridge and park by the road. Follow the signs to the spring; go up the river for larger pools (42.8192, 13.5474 and 42.8176, 13.5437).

15 mins easy, 42.8220, 13.5475

Lago di Fiastra

128

126 Bomba

126

128

The small village of Pietraferrazzana, perched beneath a towering cliff in a panoramic position, is certainly worth a visit, as well as Pennadomo and Colledimezzo. At the southern end of Lago di Bomba, visit Villa Santa Maria, a town surrounded by large sandstone, clay and limestone rocks, set back in a panoramic position, and known for its famous chefs. Some of the waterfalls here make excellent jacuzzis **127**.

Continue west to Pescocostanzo, a small town located in the province of L'Acquila. Walking in the old town is like taking a trip back in time 500 years, with its many Renaissance and Baroque monuments and churches, such as the stunning Collegiata di Santa Maria del Colle. North of here is the Parco Nazionale della Majella, the wildest and most rugged area of the central Apennines, where wolves and bears still survive, in wild canyons dotted with monasteries and abbeys. The valley of the River Orta is a beautiful example. Here you will walk beside turquoise and emerald sparkling waters, with numerous beaches where you can stop, but the real attraction is Cisterna del Fiume Orta **128**, a natural pool carved into the rock, located about two metres above the level of the river under a small waterfall. It's great to relax ▶

© Torrente Lavino

Sangro and Orta Valleys

126 LAGO DI BOMBA

This long lake is surrounded by pretty villages perched on the mountains. The shores are a mixture of sand and stone, with plenty of lush green grass to sunbathe on. Places to camp are easily found along the banks, or you can sleep in the tourist centre, Isola Verde (www.isolaverdeonline.it). The western shore terrain is wild, so we recommend visiting it on foot or mountain bike.

→ From the SS652 travelling S, take the S exit at Colledimezzo, and exit following the sign for Pietraferrazzana. Turn R at the junction, then take first L after about 1.5km towards the lake. Cross the level-crossing and follow the road to the sign 'Aquatica.' Turn L and park, walk down to lake.

→ 5 mins easy, 41.9880, 14.3684

127 VILLA SANTA MARIA

The waters of the Sangro make their way through giant boulders smoothed over time, forming pools and waterfalls all under a massive rock. It's really worth taking a peek at. The large lake is perfect for swimming and diving, and the waterfalls make excellent jacuzzis. If this location is busy, you will find many other beautiful lakes and small, isolated pools up the river.

→ From Colledimezzo, take the SS652 SW and exit at Montelapiano/Villa Santa Maria. Bear right after the first bridge and park on R just past the second. Take the narrow alley on the L between the two shops just after the bridge. Walk until you see the sign for the beach. From the beach you can go up the river, past the big rock on your R.

→ 13 mins easy, 41.9462, 14.3469

128 LA CISTERNA DEL FIUME ORTA

The valley of the river Orta abounds in picturesque spots with tranquil, natural pools. There are many other beaches and pools 500m upstream, where you can find places to dive from.

→ From Pescara take A25 dir Sulmona. Exit at Torre dè Passeri and keeping R, follow Salle for Bolognano, taking third exit L at roundabout. In Bolognano, turn L to the church and leave your car. Walk down the narrow road on the L where you will see a wooden sign stating 'La cisterna'. Follow the path down to the riverbed, and then head upstream. Keep your eyes peeled; the cisterna is not very visible as it remains approximately 2m above you on your L.

30 mins moderate, 42.2126, 13.9652

129 TORRENTE LAVINO

Springs and pools of incredible colours and sulphur ponds lie among ancient willows and magical poplars. This area is protected, but follow the river to find small pools in which to swim. Near an old mill up the river there is a very popular spot for diving.

→ Exit the A25 at Alanno-Scafa, and turn R onto the SS5. Turn L towards Decontra. After 2km turn R signed 'Parco Lavino/sorgenti sulfuree'. Continue until you find a car park on your L with a small statue and shelter. From there you will find the path that leads to the river.

5 mins easy, 42.2441, 14.0190

Villa Santa Maria, upper pool

127

127

131A

131A

130 Lago di San Domenico

here, surrounded by the lush, tropical greenery and giant boulders. Not far away from here is the Lavino springs park **129**. This area is protected, but the lush turquoise waters are perfect to laze by in the shade of the willows and poplars, making it a captivating experience.

Heading south-west, you will find the fantastic gorges of Sagittario, a narrow and deep canyon carved in limestone that always fascinates its visitors. This is an area of considerable ecological importance, which offers spectacular views from road that climbs up its slopes.

The road that leads to the Lago di Scanno passes L'Eremo di San Domenico, now protected and enclosed by a small church. Passing the small porch in front of the church, you reach a beautiful, wild beach **130**. 5 minutes away you will find the quiet Lago di Scanno, heart-shaped when viewed from the south, and cupped by mountains. Its water is clean and warm, a perfect invitation for a long swim **131**. A little further upstream is the picturesque village of Scanno itself, also worth a stop.

The final stop is Roccamandolfi, in the province of Isernia in the region of Molise. Here, at the foot of a magnificent fortress, perched on top of a hill behind a tower, you will find a beautiful gorge where the Torrente Callora flows between waterfalls and blue pools; not easy to reach, but charming **132**.

Upper Valley of Sagittario and Roccamandolfi

130 LAGO DI SAN DOMENICO

This enchanting lake is the perfect showcase for the dramatic views of the Gole del Sagittario. A green spot between high rocks and mountains, in a gorge where the sun sets beautifully each evening, adding a touch of mystery perfect for a romantic evening. The beach is surrounded by nature, and is not far from the hermitage. The wooden tables make it an ideal spot for a picnic.

→ Leave the A25 at Cocullo and follow the Via Santa Maria in Campo to join the SS479 going S. After about 7km, you will reach Lago di San Domenico. Stop 500m beyond the dam and cross the bridge to the hermitage of San Domenico. Go past the hermitage and down to the beach. A small walk leads you to the beautiful small spring Sega, and continuing on this path you will reach the village of Villalago.

5 mins easy, 41.9421, 13.8277

131 LAGO DI SCANNO

A Villalago

Public beach with a beautiful lawn and a gravel bank. There is a kiosk with pedal boats available to hire ⛵. The heart-shaped lake is surrounded by stunning mountains, and the old village of Scanno can't be missed.

From Lago di San Domenico continue S on the SS479, which will take you to the Lago di Scanno. Turn R toward the Camping I Lupi and park by the T junction at the end of the road. ⛺ Campsite I Lupi, is on a natural terrace with a beautiful view of the lake just 100m from a small beach (Tel 0864 740 625).

20 mins moderate, 41.9229, 13.8575

B Hotel Park

A large beach in front of the Hotel Park, with beautiful views of the lake and the surrounding mountains.

→ Instead of turning R at the end of the lake as above, continue on the SS479 S for a two mins longer and you will find the hotel on your L. Park in front of the hotel.

3 mins easy, 41.9234, 13.8656

132 TORRENTE CALLORA

The most beautiful parts of this gorge, with many waterfalls, are only reachable with canyoning equipment, but other areas can be reached quite easily. In very dry summers you may not find any water.

A Il Ponte

→ Exit for Roccamandolfi from the SS17. Continue for 7km and park near the bridge on the hairpin bend over the river Callora. You will find wooden signs from which the Fringuelli trail departs. After a fairly easy first part, where you will come to several pools, the path becomes challenging.

15 mins hard, 41.4972, 14.3512

B La Rocca

→ Continue along Via Santa Maria and turn R towards Longano after Roccamandolfi. After about 1km, park at the start of a path R up to a castle. Walk up the small road a little further on and you will see a rope bridge leading to the river. 🍴 Eat at Agriturismo La Curea.

1 mins moderate, 41.4952, 14.3436

Campania

In this wild green area, just a short distance away from the spectacular Amalfi coast, you'll find breathtaking rocky canyons with freshwater pools, streams and sparkling waterfalls to bathe in.

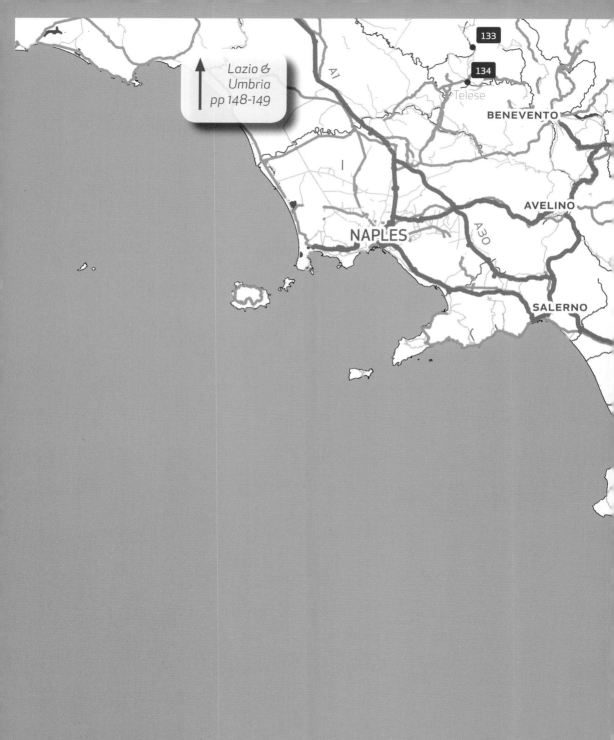

Lazio &
Umbria
pp 148-149

133

134

Telese

BENEVENTO

A1

A30

AVELINO

NAPLES

SALERNO

Highlights
Campania

Our favourites include:

136 Sorgenti del Sammaro - swim up into the narrow gorge, through crystal-clear cold water, and discover the river's source. A magic and fascinating place

138 Gole di Felitto – a network of five gorges. Rent a canoe, follow the trails or swim your way into the inner depths.

140 Forra dell'Emmisi - a secluded, enclosed gorge overhanging with lush greenery

142 Cascata Capelli di Venere – stand beneath this mossy waterfall which pours over a cave into a turquoise pool

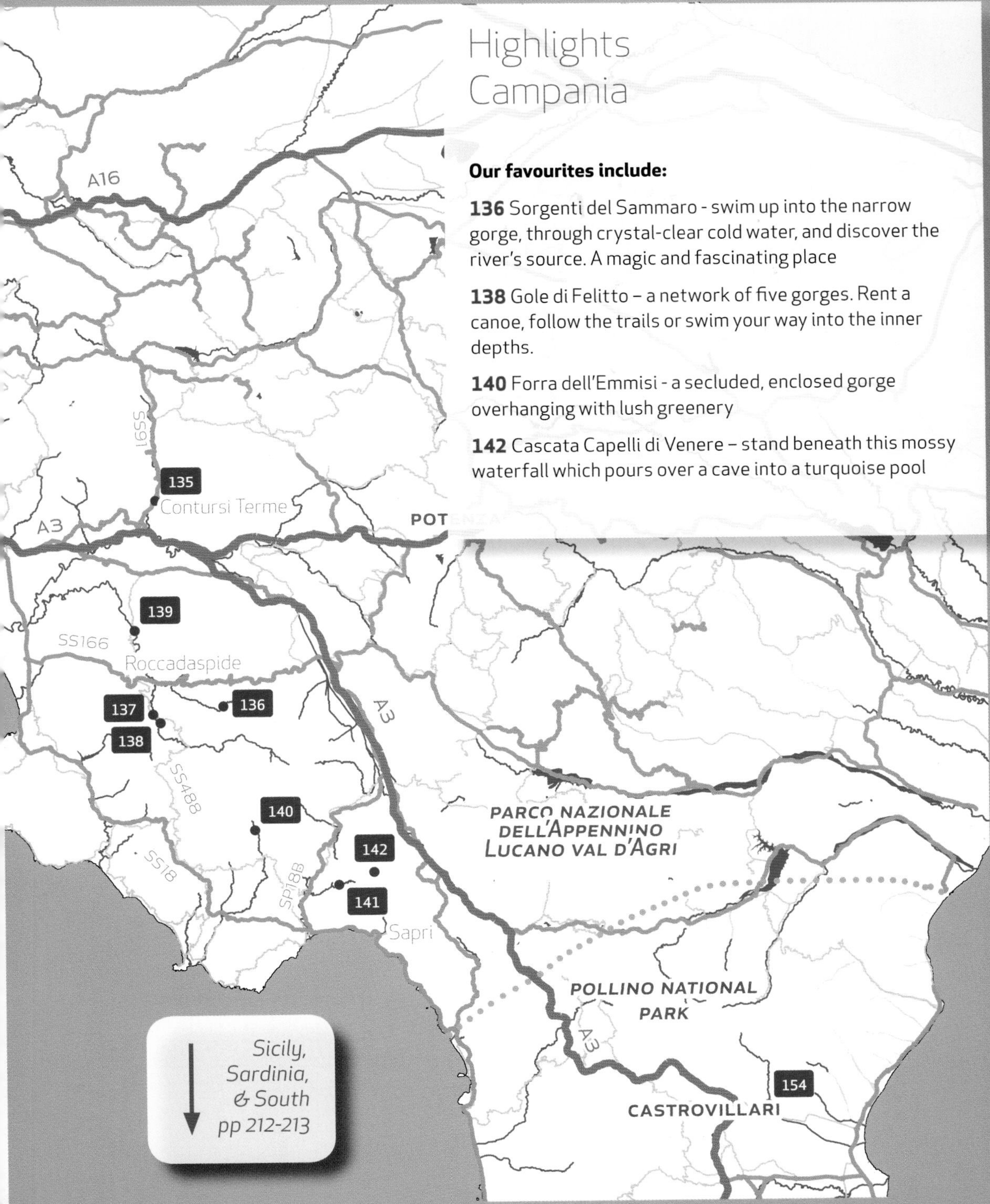

A16

SS91

135
Contursi Terme

A3

POTENZA

139

SS166
Roccadaspide

137
138
136

SS488

SS18

A3

140

SP188

142

141

Sapri

PARCO NAZIONALE
DELL'APPENNINO
LUCANO VAL D'AGRI

POLLINO NATIONAL
PARK

A3

154

CASTROVILLARI

Sicily,
Sardinia,
& South
↓
pp 212-213

135

This part of southern Italy is a land of high cliffs plunging into the deep blue sea, secluded beaches and clear natural pools. The best known areas of Campania are Naples, Capri and the ancient Greek temples in Salerno, but we advise you turn your back to the sea and the crowds of tourists in the cities. Head to the mountains instead, among villages clinging precariously to the rocks, and with superb sunset views, on an adventure to hunt out the best swim spots nature has to offer. Blue pool springs, clear water gorges and sparkling waterfalls all await your exploration.

Begin at the Fiume Titerno 133 in the Parco Regionale del Matese, near the town of Cerreto Sannita in Benevento, where you will find a rocky stream under the Roman bridge, the Ponte di Annibale. There's also a small pebble bank and a path leads along the right hand bank down to smaller pools. ▶

134

River Sele and soure of the Sammaro

133 FIUME TITERNO

A beautiful stream nestled among the rocks under the Ponte di Annibale near Cerreto Sannita. To the left of the bridge there's a small pebble bank, and to the right there's a path that runs along the river and leads to other smaller pools.

→ From Telese (20km NW of Benevento), take the SP10 towards Cerreto Sannita. Pass the town and continue on the SP12 for 1km, stopping next to a metal scultpure depicting Hannibal's elephants with spears. Walk down the concrete road on the R of the statue, to the lookout point where you will see the Ponte di Annibale.

5 mins easy, 41.2919, 14.5494

134 LAGO DI TELESE

A small lake with beautiful blue waters. You will find a small beach next to a bar called Miralago, and a grassy lawn to relax on.

→ The lake is easily accessible from either Benevento or Caserta. From the SS87 at the eastern end of Telese, head NW on Via Bagni Vecchi, following the signs into Telese. After 750m turn L onto Via Turistica del Lago, follow it S through the town, between the vineyard and olive grove and you will arrive at the lake. Follow the one-way road around to the parking area at the lake's north shore.

1 min easy, 41.2129, 14.5350

135 FIUME SELE, CONTURSI TERME

Two pools separated with beautiful rocky beaches and large boulders. At the rear there's a picnic area with tables and barbeque. Unfortunately this pool is not as clean as the rest in the park.

→ From the A3, exit at Contursi Terme, then exit the SS691 at Contursi Terme Est. Turn R at the T junction and go straight over the crossroads. After 150m, park near a gate on the R, where a pedestrian area begins. Follow the white road S on foot for 100m, passing the area with picnic tables, and from there take the steps.

5 mins easy, 40.6716, 15.2457

136 SORGENTI DEL SAMMARO

Magnificent blue-coloured pools and smooth rocks, rising from underground springs, hidden near the entrance of a narrow gorge. Swim into the gorge from the main pool. The water is clear and cold. Dive down and swim among the beams of light. Simply spectacular.

→ Travel four junctions (30km) SE of Contursi Terme (above) and leave the A3 at Atena Lucana. Follow signs to Polla and at the roundabout go straight over and continue for 20km on the SS166. On a hairpin bend bear L towards Roscigno, and then towards Sacco. Cross the Ponte di Sammaro, mid-way between Roscigno and Sacco, go on 1km and then turn R in Via Piano della Monaca. Park at the third bend where a dirt road begins (signed 'Sorgenti del Sammaro' but not easy to spot). Take the road down to the river. Do not cross the river but take the path on your R, before the bridge.

30 mins easy, 40.3880, 15.3622

138

137

138

A short journey south, roughly 15 kilometres, brings you to the city of Telese Terme, which means 'sapphire hot springs'. The remains of Roman baths here remind you why. Just south, near the valley of the Fiume Calore, there's the Lago di Telese 134. It has vivid azure waters in which to swim.

Head south 100 kilometres, beyond Naples and Salerno, to refresh yourself in the village of Contursi Terme, at the Fiume Sele 135. It's just a few minutes off the A3 autoroute and there are two milky blue pools hidden among the rocks and greenery with a picnic area adjacent.

Now you are only two steps away from the amazing Parco Nazionale del Cilento, Vallo di Diano e Alburni. This one of Italy's greatest parks, and an untouched treasure awaiting exploration. Make sure you visit the Sorgenti del Sammaro (source of the Sammaro) near the village of Roscigno 136, a few junctions down from Contursi Terme. The spring rises within the narrow, sculpted gorges, creating super-clear pools that are freezing but perfect for a therapeutic plunge. Not far away, the abandoned village of Roscigno Vecchio is filled with charm. Deserted about a century ago due to the frailty of the land, it forced the inhabitants to build new houses in the lower area of the village, leading to the legend of the 'walking village'. ▶

Castelcivita

River Calore

137 PONTE MEDIEVALE, FELITTO

A blue pool nestled between jagged rocks, with a medieval stone bridge soaring above. From here you can see the spectacular lower part of the Gole di Felitto, but watch out for currents as the gorge is narrow and the flow can be strong.

→ From Felitto, head NW on SS488. Park before the road bridge (from here you can look N to see the medieval bridge below). You can go down to the river from the dirt track by the sign just past the parking area. Bearing R you will arrive at the bridge, or go L towards the river bed. There is also a trail along the hillside (not often by the water) towards Remolino (swim 138), taking about 90 minutes and passing the beautiful 'Marmitte dei Giganti' (giant plunge pools).

5 mins moderate , 40.3776, 15.2386

138 GOLE DI FELITTO, REMOLINO

A series of spectacular rocky, narrow gorges upstream of Felitto. There's a wonderful natural pool and beach, and grassy areas with basic camping. You can also rent canoes to explore the first part of the gorge, as far as the weir. You can swim and explore up into the gorges or follow the path along the river as far as the medieval bridge of Magliano (4-5 hours).

→ From Felitto head upstream E on the SS488. Take the first R once out of the village and follow the signs for 'Gole del Calore'. Turn R again at a crossroads with a dead end straight on, and R again at a fork on a bend where Remolino is also signed. When you reach Remolino picnic area, park and follow the gravel path leading to the river. Oasis Remolino has basic ⛺ camping facilities and 🛶 canoes. The first pools are easy to reach, but you can also go up through the gorges on a 4–5 hour challenging hike.

5 mins easy, 40.3659, 15.2513

139 FIUME CALORE, CASTELCIVITA

A bend in the Fiume Calore here is tight enough to slow the flow of water and create two deep pools. Inside the bend, a pebble beach is ideal for sunbathing, while there are grassy areas on the other side that offer shade. Behind the beach there are two picnic areas that you have to pay to use, while the beach itself is free. It is often crowded and noisy, but can be quiet on the right days.

→ The beaches are easily reached from the SS488. About 2km south of Controne, cross the Ponte di Spartaco. After about 250m you will find a small sign on your R indicating the 'Fiume Calore Area Pic-Nic' off to the left. You can park for free in some areas (leave enough room for the buses). You have to pay a fee to park in the picnic area, while crossing it to get to the river does not cost anything. Tables can be rented. The river bank is also accessible by taking the next turning towards the picnic area 'Pugliese' in. Here you will find barbeque facilities.

2 mins easy, 40.4929, 15.2068

138 Castelcivita

140 Forra dell'Emmisi

141

140

From Roscigno, a circuitous route via the SS166 brings you to the village of Felitto, famous for its hand-rolled fusilli pasta, for which they hold the Sagra del Fusillo festival every August. Here in the valley of the Fiume Calore you will find many rocky beaches and gorges. The Ponte Medievale **137** is a medieval stone bridge with a pool below. From here you can look down towards the lower chambers of the Gole di Felitto, where the Fiume Calore winds through the final of its five gorges. Or walk upstream passing the beautiful 'Marmitte dei Giganti' (deep pools), towards Remolino **138**. This upstream area, also accessible by car, is great from swimming or canoeing and allows you to experience the gorge safely. Spend the night in the woods or at Oasis Remolino, an area with basic facilities, and in the morning begin exploring the gorges; it can take a good 4–5 hour hike to see them all. We spent the night in the woods here and in the morning the silence was surreal, the stillness of the forest interrupted only by the sound of water and birdsong.

Rather different in character is the broad sunlit surface of the pools at Castelcivita **139**, just 10 kilometres to the north. Although they can be busy, their shelving pebble beaches and easy access make them good for families. Make the next leg of your journey to southern Cilento and head to the town of ▶

Forra dell'Emmisi

142

142

142

Rofrano, and the Forra Dell'Emmisi 140, a long gorge with water as clear as glass. It has a rock beach where you can picnic in the shade of oaks and alders. The light filters through the branches, making the water shimmer, but it can be shady. The sheer cliffs of the canyon continue for about 500 metres, topped by trees, and are home to other pools of different sizes.

From the village of Morigerati, 35 kilometres south, is Rio Bussentino 141, with its small pebbly beach spanned by two stone bridges, which perfectly frame the scene. You can swim up the river, but watch out for the currents if the flow is strong. The Bussento caves make a magical excursion from here, with an old mill and springs that rise from a mysterious grotto. Swimming there is forbidden.

Before you end your journey in this region, you must head east from Morigerati towards the town of Casaletto Spartano, to see the Cascata Capelli di Venere 142, a waterfall named the 'Hair of Venus', made up of innumerable delicate cascades of water. This is a truly spectacular spot to swim, so plunge in and cool down under the fast-flowing rivulets of the small waterfall, which flows over a cave covered with moss. You will leave fully enchanted and certainly ready to plan a return visit.

142 Cascata Capelli di Venere

Southern Cilento

140 FORRA DELL'EMMISI

A 500m long, tree-lined gorge, this is not a place for sun-seekers, but the light that does filter through creates green patterns on the crystal waters – this is a magical place to be. There's a rock 'beach' at the beginning and plenty of pools to swim in.

→ From Salerno, follow the A3 southbound and exit at Buonabitacolo. At the roundabout take the second exit, merge onto the SS517 and take the exit for Sanza. Go through the town centre and take the SP18b towards Rofrano. Pass through it to the SP18a, and about 1.5km after leaving the village, note a wooden signboard on the right indicating the beginning of a path. Park at the next bend, walk back to the signboard and go down to the river.

2 mins easy, 40.2156, 15.4158

141 RIO BUSSENTINO, MORIGERATI

This is a wonderfully picturesque place for a swim, with a large river pool flowing under two old stone bridges. There's a pebbly beach at the mouth of the ravine where you can relax, although you might want to bring something softer to sit on. You can swim up the river, but you will have to watch out for currents as they can vary, depending on the electricity company's use of the water.

→ From Salerno, take the A3 southbound, exit at Buonabitacolo/Padula and follow the signs to Buonabitacolo. At the roundabout take the second exit and merge onto the SS517 and continue for 23km, then take the SP210 for Sicili. Turn L on to the SP54 for Morigerati but, before the village, you will find a small bridge over the river Bussentino. Park your car and go down the small path on the left that you will find at the beginning of the bridge.

2 mins easy, 40.1388, 15.5635

142 CASCATA CAPELLI DI VENERE

Stand beneath a waterfall of a thousand golden rivulets lit by the sun, flowing over a cave covered with moss, into a turquoise pool surrounded by lush greenery. From the car park another path goes further downstream, leading to a bend with other beautiful pools to explore. There are quiet places where you can pitch your tent ⛺. If you walk up the slope of the hill above the pool, you will find a picnic area.

→ Return to the SS517 from Sicili, and head north, following signs for Caselle in Pittari. Once in the village take the SP16 towards Casaletto Spartano, after which you will come to a bridge with a fountain at its end. Park a few metres further on the right and walk back towards the fountain. From there a short path leads you to the waterfall. Below the house on your right you will see t two picnic tables.

2 mins easy, 40.1566, 15.6258

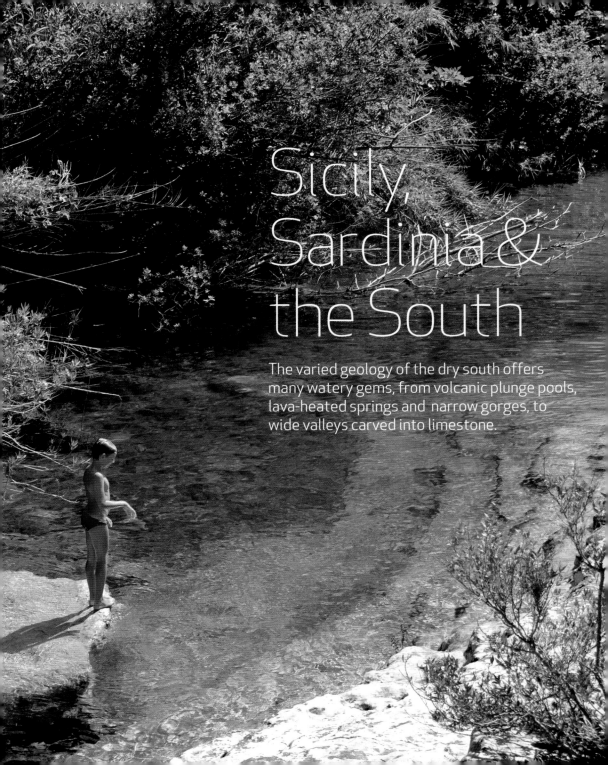

Sicily, Sardinia & the South

The varied geology of the dry south offers many watery gems, from volcanic plunge pools, lava-heated springs and narrow gorges, to wide valleys carved into limestone.

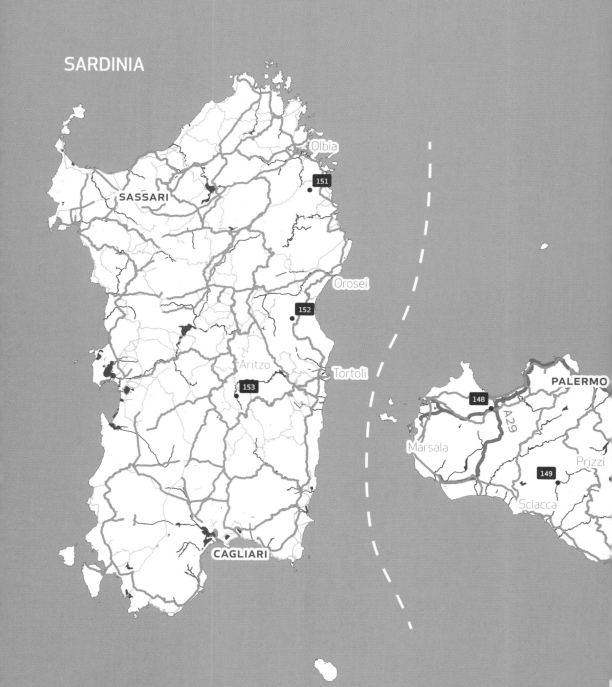

SARDINIA

Olbia

151

SASSARI

Orosei

152

Aritzo

Tortoli

153

CAGLIARI

PALERMO

Marsala

A29

148

Prizzi

149

Sciacca

Highlights
Sicily, Sardinia & South

↑ *Campania pp 196-197*

Our favourites include:

143 Gole dell'Alcantara – swim into the gorge through extraordinary basalt volcanic rock formations

146 Pantalica – this huge canyon necropolis contains thousands of ancient rock tombs. Descend to the wooded valley bottom for magnificent plunge pools, some of the best in the region

147 Cavagrande del Cassibile - one of our favourite places in Italy, a flower-filled canyon with many pools and waterfalls

151 Gola di Gorropu - a spectacular limestone canyon where you swim in the shadow of 500m high cliifs

152 Sa Stiddiosa – deep in the wild heart of Sardinia, this lush deep gorge is lined with dripping moss and verdant waterfalls

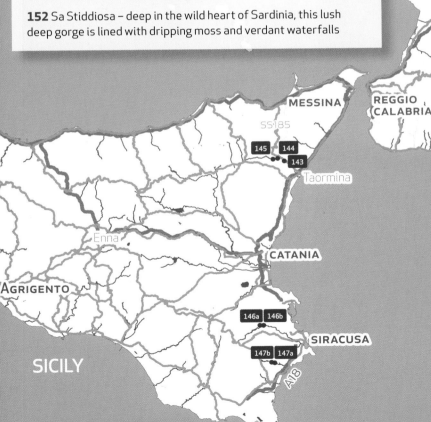

143 Gole dell'Alcantara

The extraordinary range of landscapes in the wild south of Italy and its islands will take away anyone's breath. Small villages cling to rocks, verdant valleys are cloaked by forest, and sunny canyons await yielding secret pools and waterfalls.

Begin your trip in the far south, in Sicily. With some of the most beautiful flora in the Mediterranean, there is spectacular scenery all around. A rich architectural heritage has been left by many invaders. The seven temples of the Valle dei Templi in Agrigento and the amphitheatre and temple of Segesta are just two great sites where the ancient Greeks left their stamp on the surrounding landscape.

A walk on Mount Etna on the east coast of Sicily brings home how small we are in relation to nature, and is a taster for what awaits in the valley of the Alcantara river. Here, in the Gole

▶

The Alcantara Gorges, north-east Sicily

143 GOLE DELL'ALCANTARA

A narrow gorge, no more than 4–5m wide, its walls made up of great basaltic prisms stacked one on top of the other, rising to a height of 25m. The water is clear but cold, and the sun just filters in, creating beautiful plays of light on the dark walls. The first part of the gorge is easy to explore. Further downstream large boulders create rapids, waterfalls and other small pools. Approximately 500m downstream a wide and sunny beach will help you warm up after your swim.

→ From Taormina, take the A18/E45 S and exit at Giardini Naxos; taking the SS185 NW towards Francavilla di Sicilia. Continue for 13km to the Parco Botanico e Geologico delle Gole dell'Alcantara. As you approach some houses on the R, you should see lots of cars parked along the road, and you can park along this road for free. Further up on the L is the entrance to the park, which you have to pay for, but there is plenty more parking here if the road is full. You can access the river and gorge by continuing along the main road for 100m until you reach you some wooden kiosks set off the road on your R; on the opposite side there is a public stairway that leads to the gorge.
10 mins easy, 37.8799, 15.1732

144 LE GURNE

A beautiful series of 16 small, round plunge pools worn into the smooth lava bed of the river. They range from 5m to 30m across, and can reach 10m in depth. The location is picturesque, with the ruins of the Castello di Francavilla di Sicilia on the hills above. It's a pleasant walk of an hour to visit all of them.

→ From the main gorge (above), continue 4km along the SS185 to the centre of Francavilla. Turn L to take the SP7i, just after the large pink church. Follow for Randazzo/Gurne dell'Alcantara, turning L at the traffic lights into Via Liguria (signed Le Gurne); then taking the first R into Via Orsino Orsini and parking in the open space at the bottom on the L. Take the narrow road L, and then bear R. Continue straight, next to a beautiful orchard, and half way down it you will find a path on the R towards Enel (Gurna Scifazzi). Follow it to the foot bridge, but don't cross, instead head upstream. There are other pools further upstream, but they are not very easy to reach. To head downstream, go back to the main path and continue E at the mill, Chiappa, before the picnic area.
30 mins moderate, 37.8920, 15.1366

145 PICCOLE GOLE

A picturesque stretch of the river where it forms a pool, under a beautiful waterfall nestled between two walls of well-polished lava rock. The large, flat rocks act as a beach, where you can relax. Beautiful, flowering oleander grows among the rock. 300m further upstream there are two other pools, while downstream the water flows fast through the beautiful gorge.

→ From Le Gurne (above), continue along the SP7i W to the bridge on the Alcantara. Cross it and turn R and park. You will see the river ahead, upstream.
2 mins easy, 37.8886, 15.1154

144

144

Fiume Calcinara

146A

146A

dell'Alcantara **143**, the river flows between basaltic lava columns of unmatched beauty. These strange rock formations are composed of stacked pentagonal and hexagonal formations - giant crystals formed as the lava slowly cooled: a testament to the huge eruptions that have shaken this island and the molten rock that once ran through these valleys.

Further upstream you will also discover Le Gurne **144** where the river has scoured small basins out of the lava into lovely round pools. These are easily accessible in a pleasant hour's walk at the foot of the hill of the isolated Castello di Francavilla. The Piccole Gole **145** is a smaller but quieter version of the more famous gorge, but the waterfalls are impressive and make a perfect spot for the kids to paddle.

In the south-east corner of Sicily at Sortino (near Siracusa), visit the fascinating ancient necropolis at Pantalica **146**, in the narrow canyons of the Anapo and Calcinara rivers. High paths lead down into dark gorges. Over 4,000 burial chambers are carved into the rock and exude an air of solemn mystery; the sacredness of this place makes a deep impression. Your walk will bring you to the two small pools of the Fiume Anapo **146A**, where shady greenery overhangs the gorge, and the river flows from bend to bend, through little caves and ravines, creating natural pools and a ▶

146A

South-east Sicily

146 PANTALICA, SORTINO

Remote and inaccessible, this was a refuge and burial place from 1250 to 650BC. Two narrow valleys have been carved into the rock by the waters of the Anapo and Calcinara with deep canyons, tight loops and pools hidden by the dense greenery.

A Fiume Anapo

Two small pools to dive into, surrounded by luscious greenery, at the bottom of a pathsfrom the Necropolis of Pantalica trail. Ideal for cooling off after the walk.

→ From Siracusa, head NW along the SP76 to Sortino. From the S end of the town, follow Via Pantalica until it ends in a fence with a kiosk beyond. Park on the road and walk straight on to reach the first tombs. Continue and the trail descends to the valley bottom and a tiny clearing. Bear R for the river. There are some small pools here but head downstream via a rock tunnel to find the largest pool. Continue down to find the confluence with the Calcinara (below).

40 mins moderate, 37.1397, 15.0294

B Fiume Calcinara

A picturesque pool between the rocks. There are boulders which you can dive from, and a beautiful waterfall flows from a spring in the rock by the path. Following the old railway (climb up the paths that lead away from the river) you reach the pools near the tunnels (above).

→ As above, but from the road-end cross the fence on the left (via the ladder) and turn L to follow the track down to the river. Then follow the path upstream on the river's R bank.

40 mins moderate, 37.1396, 15.0353

147 CAVAGRANDE DEL CASSIBILE

10km of breathtaking canyons, walls up to 500m high, large pools carved into the rock by beautiful waterfalls. River crabs, small turtles and many birds live in this area, and the greenery is lush and filled with colourful flowers.

A Avola pools

Three beautiful pools set in the rock, separated by a waterfall. Open and sunny but can get busy.

→ From Siracusa, take A18/E45 S to the exit for Avola. Continue S along the SS115, taking the first exit at the roundabout. After about 1km turn R for Avola/Cavagrande on the SP4. Pass through Montagna and after 1.5km turn R to 'Cava Grande Laghetti' and smaller 'riserva' sign. You can park for free before the wooden cabin. The path starts from here; walk almost to the bottom of the valley and you will find a junction where you should bear R.

40 mins moderate, 36.9704, 15.1007

B Upper pools

Beautiful long pools with rocky beaches, huge boulders and fun water slides. Slightly harder to reach, and less sunny, but for these reasons they are also quieter, so enjoy the scenic walk to reach them.

→ Park as for Laghetti di Avola, but go L at the junction in the path at the bottom of the valley. The first pools are located near a ford; continue up and you will get to larger pools and water slides.

40 mins moderate, 36.9733, 15.0929

147A

147A

Avola pools, Cavagrande del Cassibile

147B

147B

149

149

149

great place to cool down. A few minutes north-east there's the Fiume Calcinara **146B**, with jade water flowing between rocks. It's an enchanting place and you should leave the trail and explore along the river for more pools.

Not far to the south-west, through the Riserva Naturale Cavagrande del Cassibile, the river Cassibile **147** has carved a deep canyon, which has been used since ancient times as both a natural means of defense and an inaccessible burial place. The Scala Cruci trail leads to the bottom of the valley, offering impressive views of the vast necropolis excavated in the rock from the 10th century BC. Down below, the river forms three large pools with waterfalls at the Avola pools **147A**. In the summer it can be busy in the canyon so - for more solitude - follow the river upstream to upper pools **147B**.

In the far north-west of Sicily (3 hours west of Siracusa) Segesta is an ancient Elymian city located on Monte Barbaro. You can visit a Doric temple from the late 5th century BC and a Greek theatre, both well-preserved with panoramic views over the valleys down to the Mediterranean and Castellammare del Golfo. At the foot of the hills by the river Caldo, hidden amongst wild grasses and tall reeds, are the Terme di Segesta **148**.

▶

149 Fiume Sosio

Western Sicily

148 TERME DI SEGESTA

These small sulphur springs, famous for thousands of years, are situated in a narrow, wild gorge surrounded by reeds and blossoming tamarisk plants. On the left bank of the river Caldo, thermal offshoots fill four pools at 47C. A brilliant place to just soak and far more therapeutic than the spa that also uses the waters. The ruins of the Castello di Calathamet can be visited on the hill above.

➜ Exit the A29/E933 at Segesta exit (about 10km W of Alcamo). On the N side of the motorway follow the SP68 / SP2 signed Castellammare and Ponte Bagni and after 7km reach Terme Segestane. Turn R for the spa but immediately on your L (after 30m) find a track which leads to a clearing where you can park. Follow the path, cross the river, turn R and you will come to the thermal pools. Continuing on you will come to other pools, with reeds and waterfalls, and still further along you will find a small pool between the thermals and a high rock.

5-10 mins easy, 37.9724, 12.8934

149 FIUME SOSIO

Turquoise tubs of water surrounded by rugged tawny cliffs, intense greenery and pink oleander flowers – remember oleander is toxic, so just look at the flowers and don't pick! The water is never too deep here, and the greenery provides shade during the hottest hours. There are plenty of rocks and small beaches for basking in the sun.

➜ From Burgio take the SS386 N. Turn R before reaching San Carlo, following the signs for Enel. Go to the viaduct and park underneath. Follow the track upstream to an intersection and continue on the trail along the river until the next ford. Walk another 300m and you will come to more pools at the beginning of a beach. You can continue the exploration to another beautiful pool (37.6391, 13.3007) another 2km, but the road is very long and not always easy.

15 mins easy, 37.6401, 13.2666

150 CAMPANARO, VALLI CUPE

A beautiful 22m waterfall, immersed in the most wonderful undeveloped natural area of Calabria, the Valli Cupe. Don't miss a visit to the mysterious canyon, in a inaccessible and rugged valley, where you can walk for hours right inside the heart of the earth,

➜ From Sersale head W to Zagarise. After 6 km park in the clearings in front of a fountain where you will find a sign indicating the start of the path to the Campanaro Waterfall (signed all the way to the waterfall). All along the Crocchio valley are great swimming holes. Visiting the whole canyon takes about 2 hours.

25 mins easy, 38.9419, 16.7516

153 Sa Stiddiosa

152

153

While you in the area do also visit Sicily's first protected area, Riserva dello Zingaro, with many untouched coves; the beautiful medieval village of Erice in Trapani, and the Saline di Marsala, which look like peaks of snow. On the south-western side of the island, towards Agrigento, the river Sosio 149 yields strange rocky outcrops with fossils and turquoise pools surrounded by lush greenery, pink flowers and blue waters. You might also visit the beautiful beach of Eraclea Minoa, where you can sleep among scented eucalyptus trees at the foot of white cliffs.

Italy's second largest island, Sardinia, is better known for its beaches than waterfalls, but in the north-east hills, above San Teodoro, the Rio Pitrisconi 150 is a wild, narrow stream ravine with shiny granite pools. From its highest 'infinity' pool you can swim right to the edge and peer over the huge waterfall below.

To the south, among the mountains of the Parco Nazionale del Golfo di Orosei e del Gennargentu, you will find the spectacular Gola di Gorropu 151, where the Rio Flumineddu cuts emerald pools through the white limestone. The walls of this awe-inspiring amazing canyon, up to 500m high, are the stuff of legends; one says that at night a rare flower blooms, with the power to make you rich. It will take a two-hour walk to reach the entrance of the gorge.

▶

Gola di Gorropu

Sardinia and Calabria

151 RIO PITRISCONI

Amazing pools overlooking magnificent waterfalls with sea views. Granite rocks glowing in shades of yellow, pink and orange, with the scent of juniper and myrtle all around.

→ From Olbia/Costa Smeralda airport, take the SS131 S for 24km; exit for San Teodoro and at the roundabout turn R towards Budoni. 1.5km later, in Budditogliu, turn R signed Aresula. Follow the road R, turn L, then go about 6km to the ranger's hut. From here you will see the trail down to the pools. Another 40mins walk will lead you to the lower, more beautiful part of the valley.

5 mins easy, 40.7504, 9.5914

152 GOLA DI GORROPU

A thrilling limestone canyon with walls up to 500m high, all carved by water. Walking between the vast boulders is a unique experience. The upper part of the canyon is equally spectacular, with snow-white limestone layers, lovely waterfalls and emerald pools.

From Dorgali take the SS125 S for Baunei. 3km after the junction to Cala Gonone, fork R down into the valley. Follow the signs until the bridge at Sa Barva. Turn L and park. Continue along the trail to the L. After 6km you will reach the gorge entrance. Along the way there are great pools to cool off in. The Sa Giuntura, an hour away, W on SS125 (40.1775, 9.4900) is equally good.

120 mins moderate, 40.1856, 9.5017

153 SA STIDDIOSA

A fantastic pool at the foot of a limestone rock, from which thin trickles of water, fed by a spring, descend. The many threads of water glisten in the sun, among a startlingly lush tropical greenery. There are more than 20 others pools along the river Flumendosa to be discovered, some less than 1km away, all with waterfalls and springs.

→ 12km S from Gadoni, on the SP8, next to a church, turn R. Follow this road and the signs 'Sa Stiddiosa'. After 4.5km, at the bottom of the valley, bear L and park before the road narrows. Follow the road

to the start of the path.

30 mins moderate, 39.8445, 9.1973

154 GOLE DEL RAGANELLO, CIVITA

A majestic gorge with waterfalls, deep pools and water slides. Downstream, small pools are formed between rocks. Much of the path is sometimes difficult, but doesn't need special equipment.

→ Exit the A3/E45 at Frascineto, turning L onto the SP263 for Civita. After 5km, turn L again for Civita. Park near the square with trees and drinking fountains. Walk to the church and take the narrow alley in front of you. From here, follow the signs 'Gole del Raganello', turning immediately R and then L into Via Piave. Follow the cobbled street downhill and then turn R towards the gorge. Take the stairs, or continue on the path. Before reaching the level of the river, a short detour to the L leads to Ponte del Diavolo for great views. Avventurieri del Sud organise guided trekking and canyoning (Tel. 329 6573757).

30 mins moderate ,39.8287, 16.3184

Gole del Raganello

154

151

Away from its famous coast, Sardinia is a wild place, ripe for waterfall explorers. Near Seulo, surrounded by lush, dripping greenery, are the magical pools, rock arches and waterfalls at Sa Stiddiosa **152** or seek out the waterfall of Sa Giuntura (see **151**).

Back on the mainland of southern Italy, pay a visit to the Parco Nazionale del Pollino, which acts as a natural geographical dividing line, separating the 'heel' from the rest of the Italian 'boot'. The park encompasses a vast mountainous area, where rocky peaks, often snow-covered, alternate with broad valleys. There are oaks, maples, beech and alder, as well as peonies, orchids and gentians. The park is home to the exquisite orange-red fire tiger lily and the magnificent Bosnian pine.

Near to Sersale, you will also find the beautiful Valli Cupe, considered one of the most beautiful natural sites in Calabria. Home to monumental trees and rich in fauna, with red walls, crevasses and towering gorges which hold many crystal-clear pools. Also visit the Gole del Raganello **153**, near the town of Civita, with 600m high canyon walls and soaring birds of prey. Finally, any enthusiast for rafting must not miss the river Lao, near Mormanno. With trips of varying difficulty, from challenging gorge descents, to quiet walks and swims in the woods, this location is ideal for the water-loving family.

Swim Maps

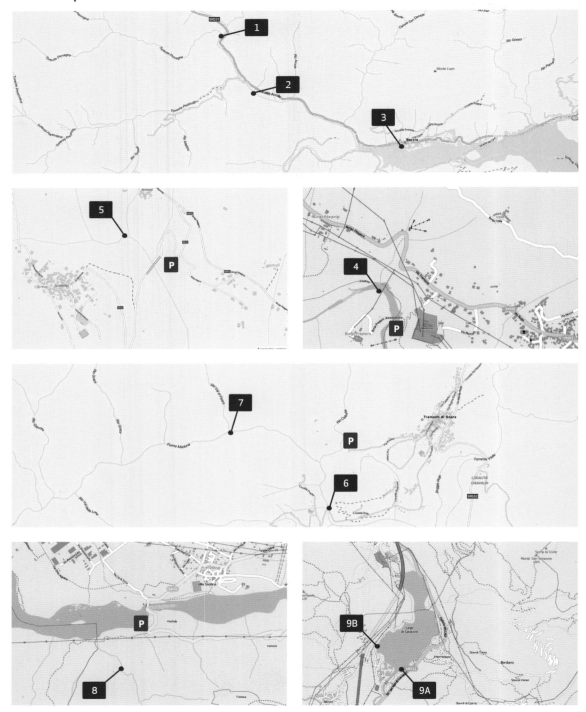

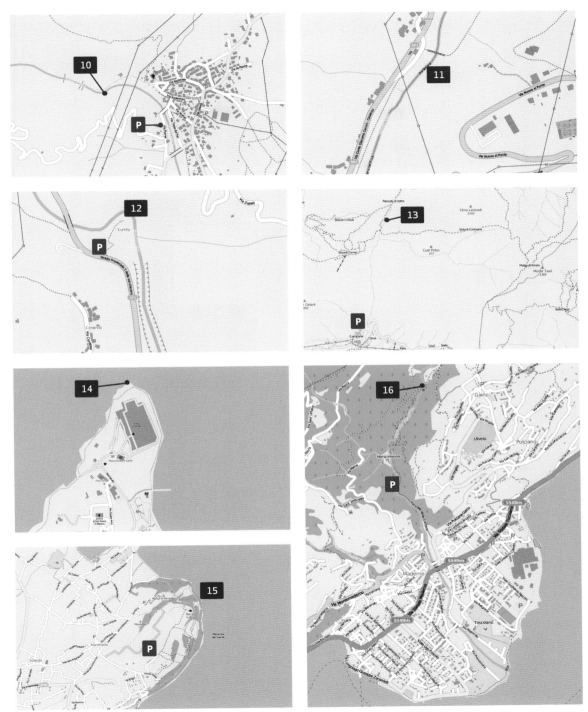

231

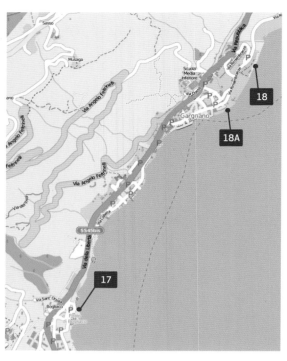

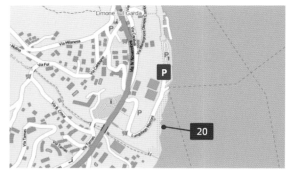

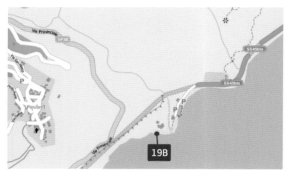

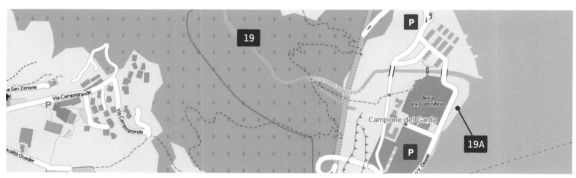

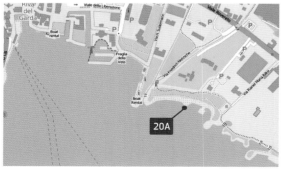

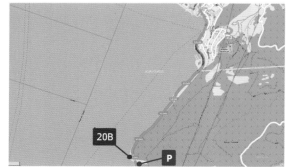

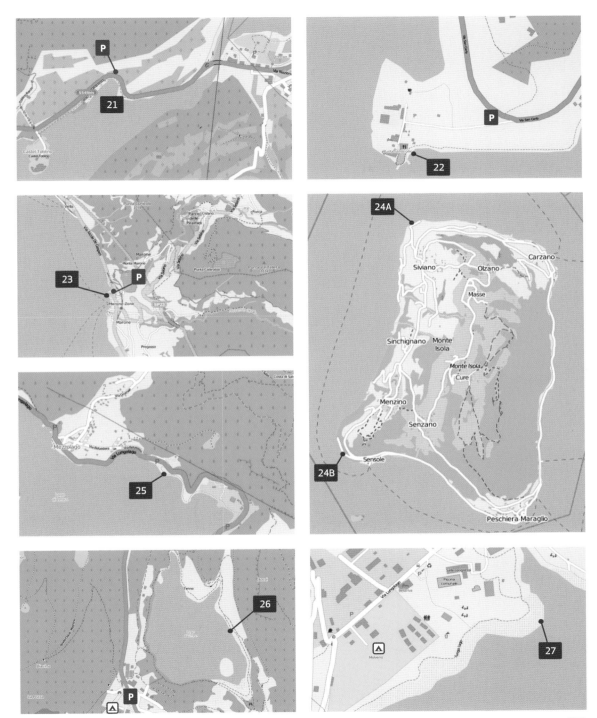

233

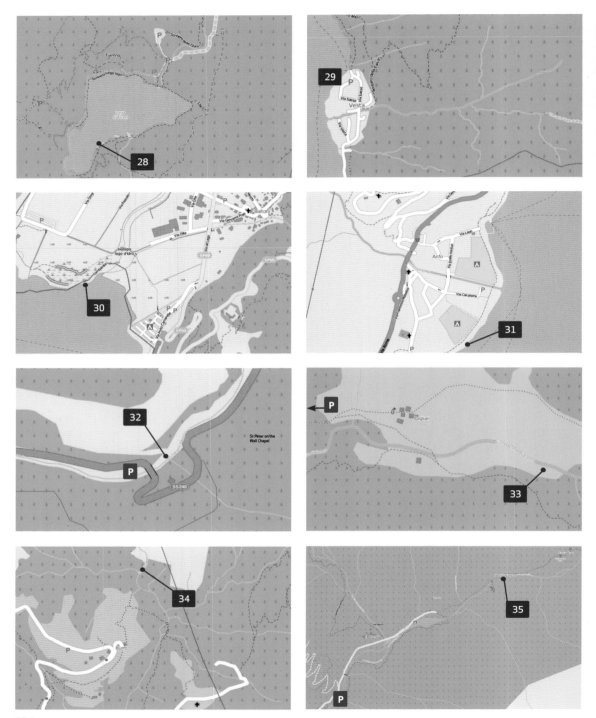

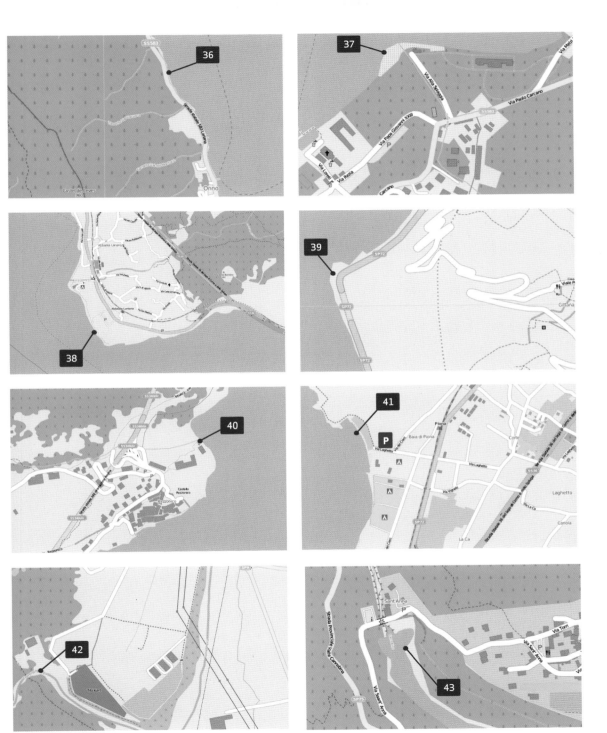

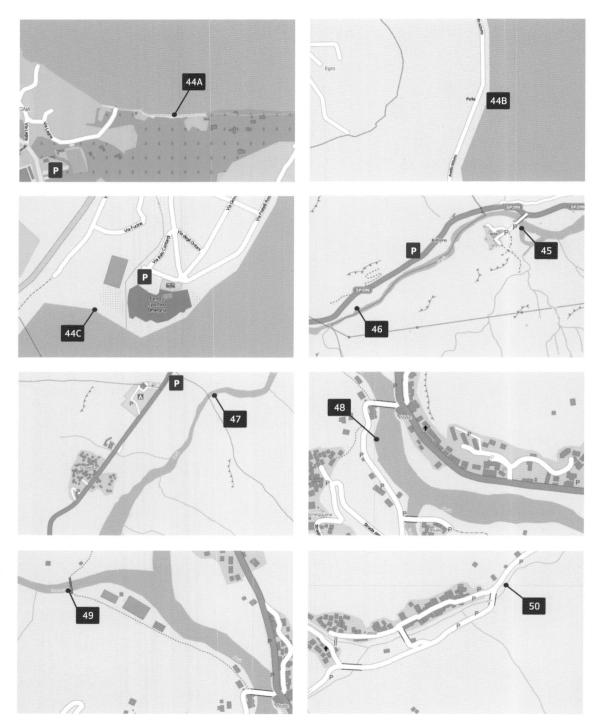

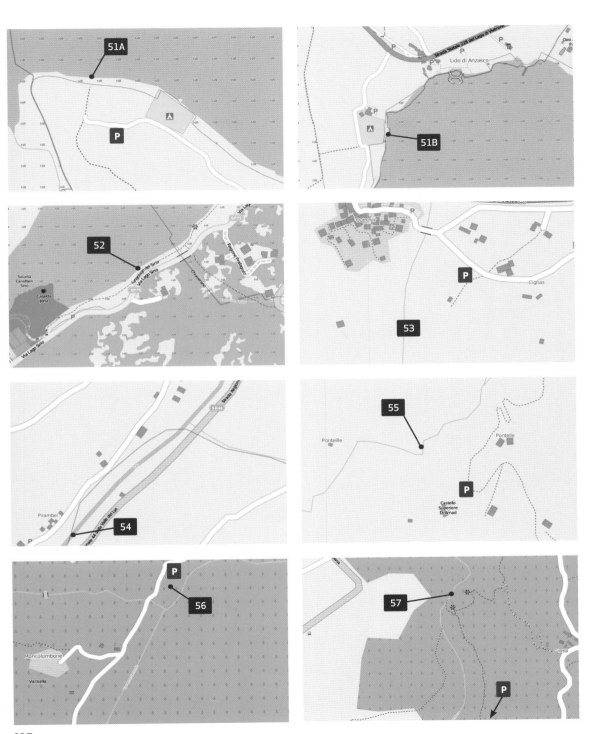

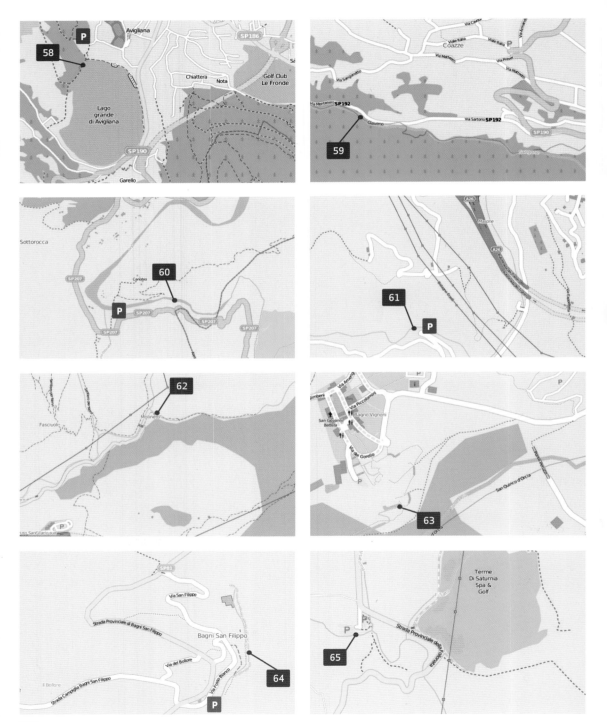

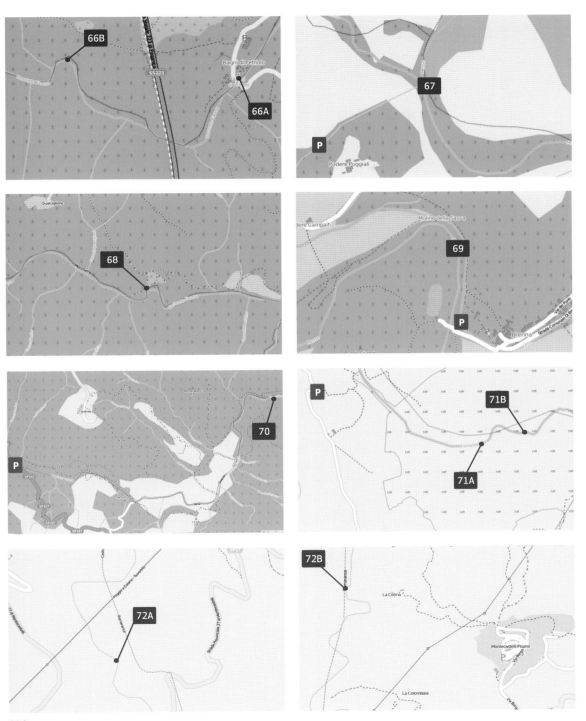

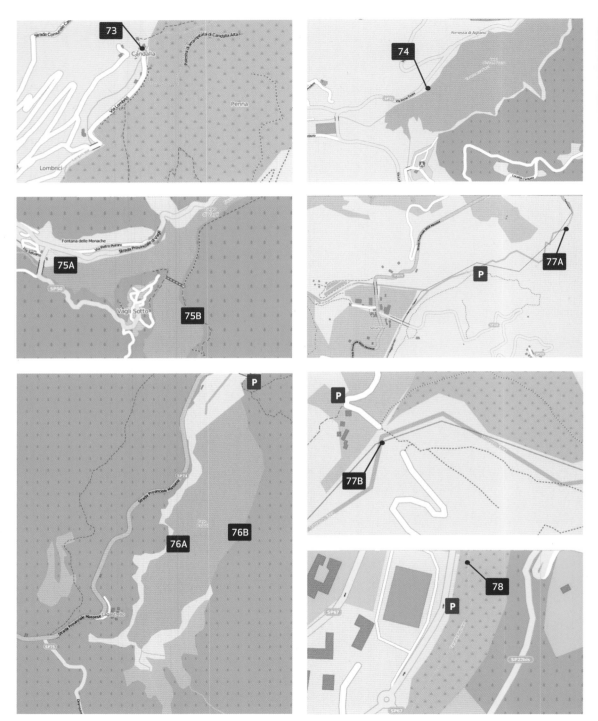

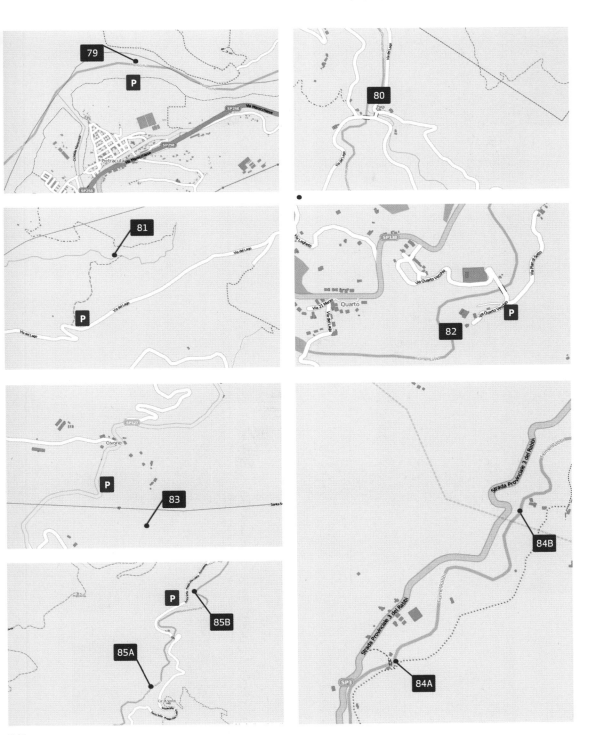

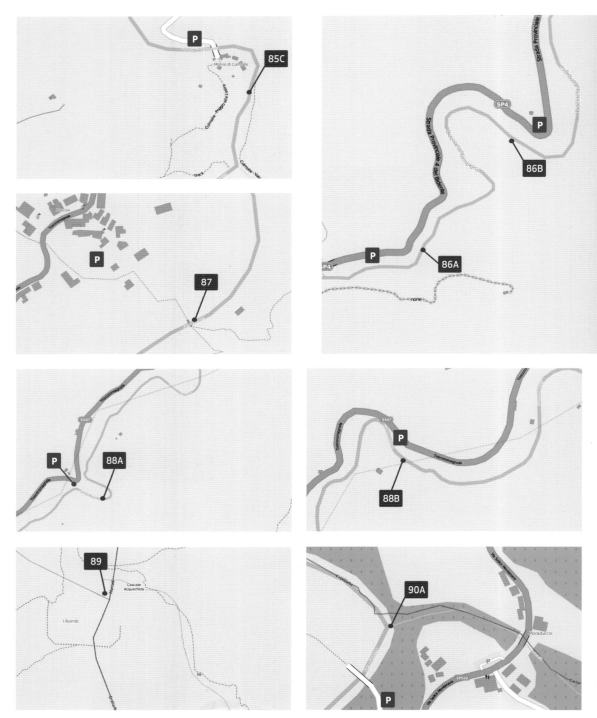

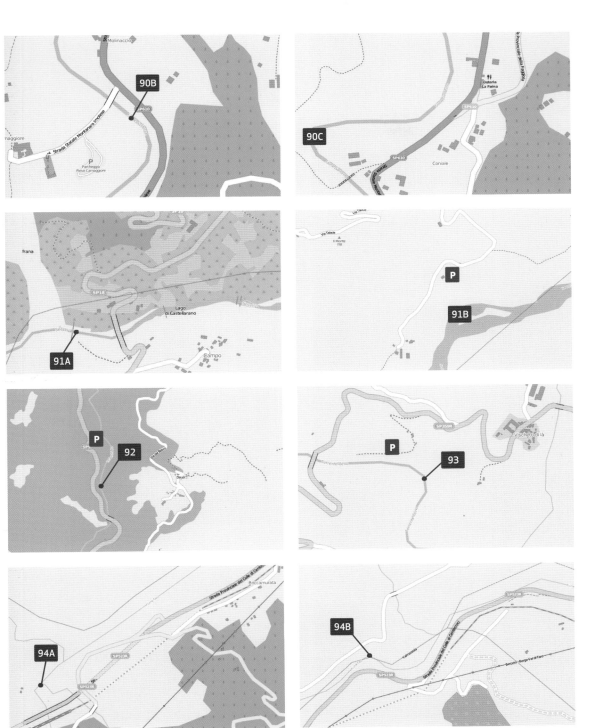

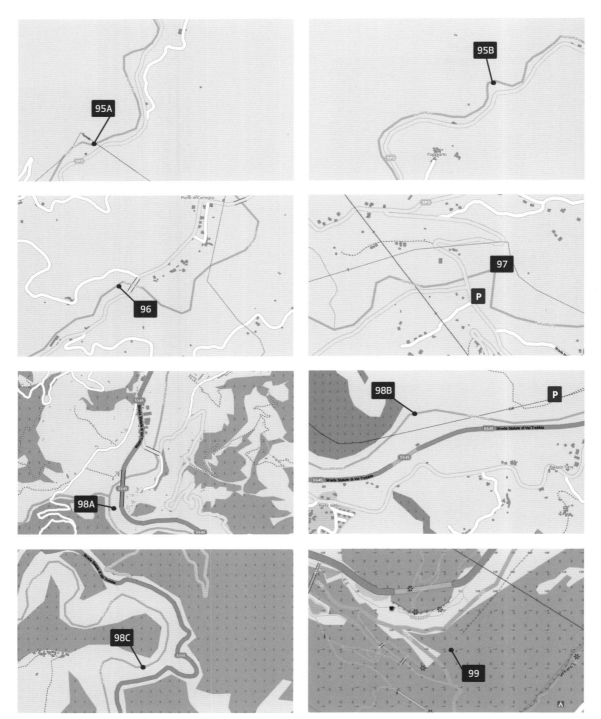

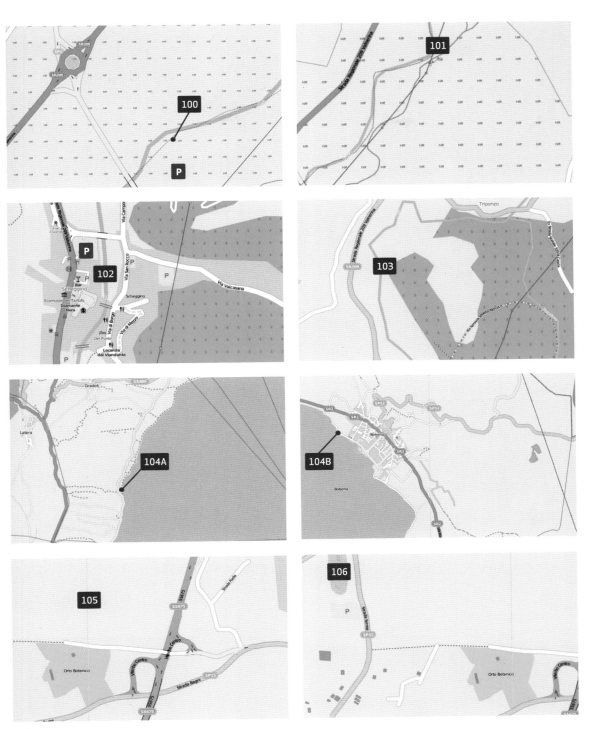

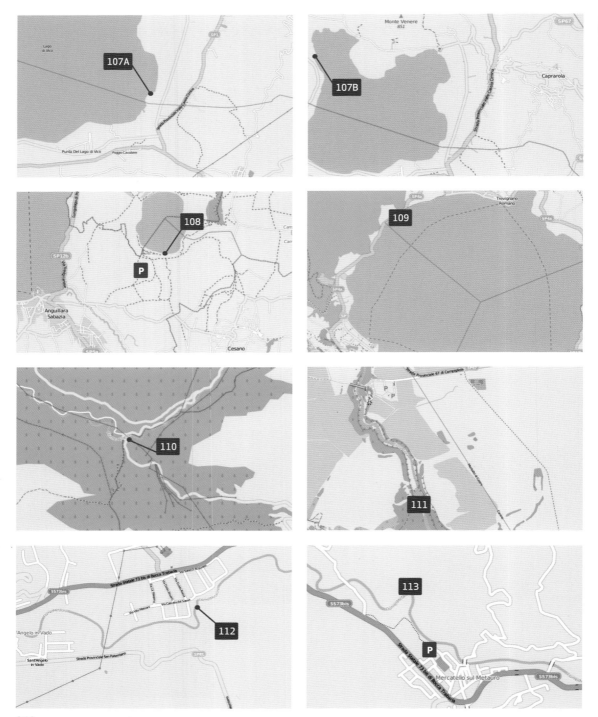

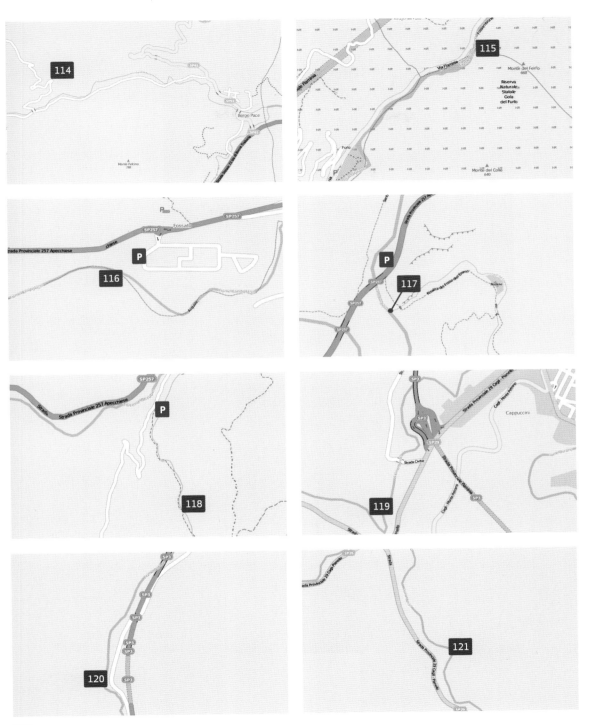

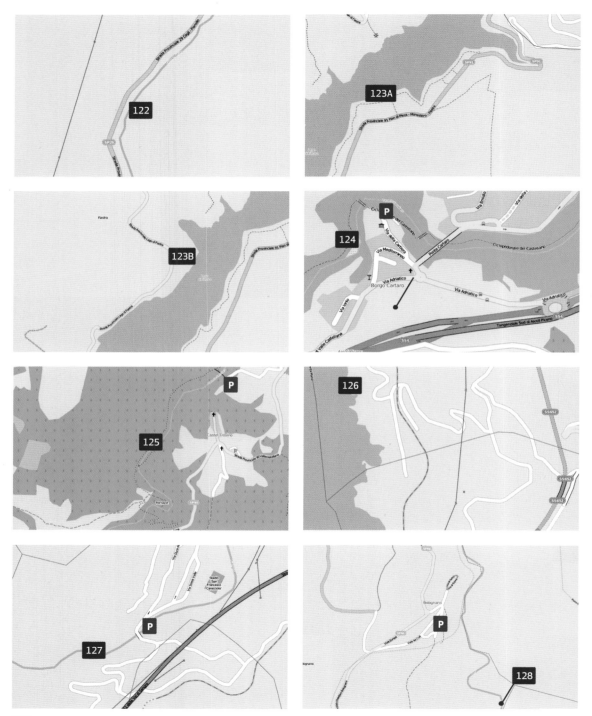

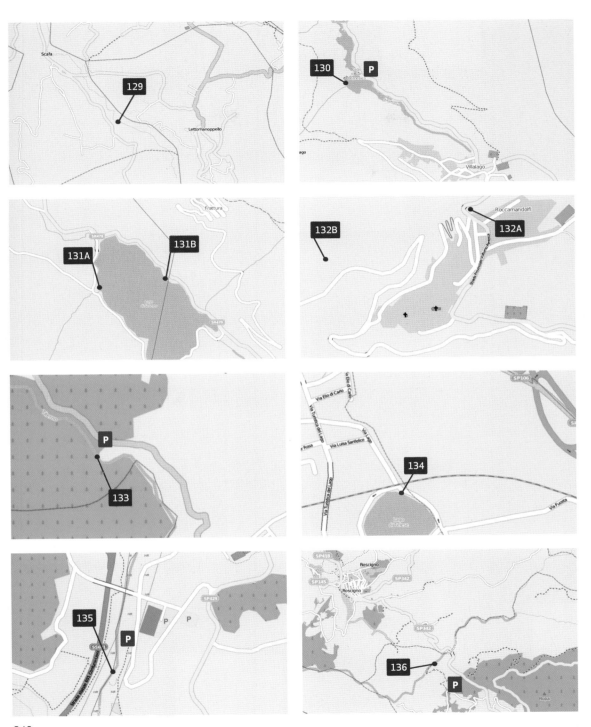

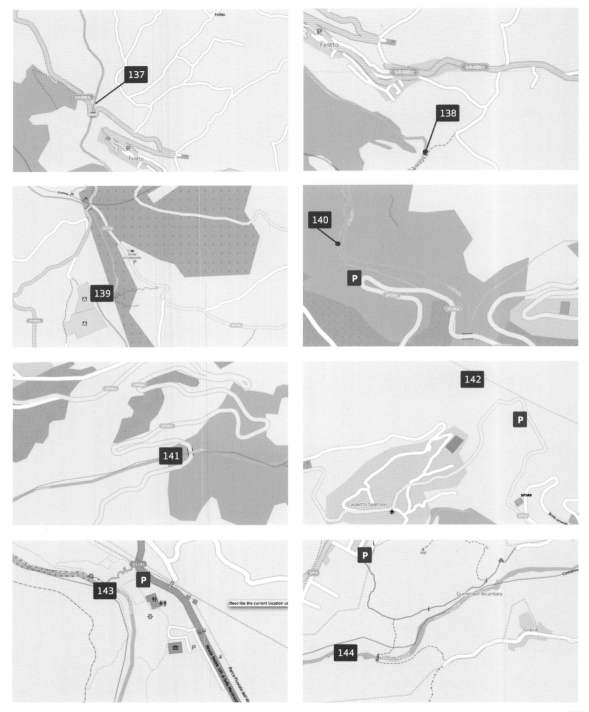

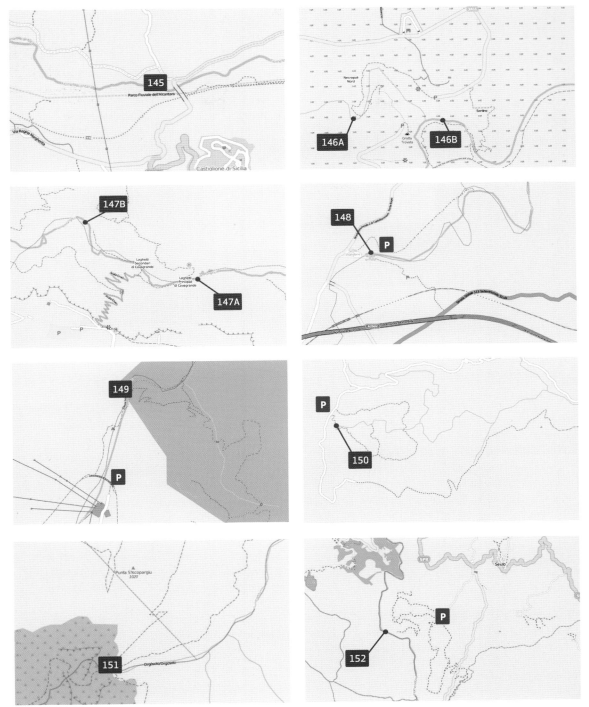

Safety and Access

Like cycling, hill-walking, canoeing and many other outdoor activities, wild swimming has some inherent risks and dangers, but with the right preparation and information you can stay very safe, without losing the sense of adventure.

Main risks

Non-swimmers and children Take special care with children and non-swimmers near water. Even shallow water can suddenly deepen. If you, your children or your friends cannot swim, make sure you scout out the extent of the shallows, set clear boundaries and maintain constant supervision. Remember that even shallow sections of fast-flowing water can knock you off your feet. Be careful with inflatables: they can create a false sense of security and float off into deep or dangerous sections, or burst. Swimmers lacking confidence should always stay close to the shore and within standing depth.

Slips, trips and falls It sounds obvious but this is the most likely hazard while clambering around in rivers and waterfalls. Wear plimsolls or jelly shoes with a rubber sole and never run or rush. If you enjoy more serious scrambling and climbing along rivers why not join a canyoning or 'acqua trekking' course?

Cold water Summer swimming in Italy is rarely cold, but out of season, or in mountain lakes or streams, the water can be bracing. Swimming in cold water saps body heat fast so don't stay in too long (20 minutes is ample). Shivering and teeth-chattering are the first stages of mild hypothermia, which can increase the risk of drowning, so get out of the water and warm up with a combination of warm, dry clothes and activity.

Jumping and diving Always check the depth of the water, even if you visit the same spot regularly. Depths can vary and new underwater obstructions - sand, rocks, branches and rubbish – may have been brought downstream overnight. Never judge water depth by just looking. A broken neck from a diving accident could paralyse you for life.

Cramps and solo-swimming Cramp most often occurs in the calf or foot. Swimming is no more likely to bring it on than any other exercise. Contrary to popular belief, cramp is not more likely to occur after eating, but dehydration, or a poor diet in general, can make you especially prone. If you regularly suffer from cramp take extra care. If you get a leg cramp, shout for help, lie on your back and paddle back to shore with your arms. For these reasons swimming alone in deep water isn't a great idea but, if you must, trail a float behind you on a cord to act as a life saver.

Weeds In slow, warm lowland rivers and lakes, weeds are quite easy to see. While one or two don't present a problem, a spaghetti-like forest could entangle a swimmer's legs, especially if they start thrashing about. Try to avoid weedy areas, but if you encounter some, don't panic, just glide through them like an eel, using your arms to paddle.

Blue–green algae In lowland lakes where the water is rich with farming fertilizers like nitrates and phosphates, algae can multiply, particularly after warm, wet weather, usually in late summer. This results in a green surface scum (the blooms) which often collect on the downwind side of a lake. It's presence is obvious and bathing in it can bring on a skin rash, irritate your eyes, and make you sick if you swallow the water. Find a part of the lake without blooms, or don't swim.

Currents Swimming with or against a current can be fun, just like swimming in seaside surf, but losing control and being carried downstream can be dangerous, especially in a rocky river. In fast-flowing water always think about where you will get out if you lose your footing and end up downstream. Identify your emergency exits before getting in and scout around for any downstream hazards (obstructions, waterfalls or weirs). In canyons, bear in mind that as the gorge narrows the water will deepen and increase in flow. Always explore canyons from the bottom up, so you can ensure there is a safe route back down again. Never enter a canyon if rain is expected in the upstream catchment.

Flooding and dam releases Italy has a large number of hydroelectric dams. These need to vary their release rates in order to meet changing electricity demands and you will see very clear triangular signs along the river where this is the case. In reality, flow rates are generally constant during the summer when electricity demand is much more predictable. Many local people swim without concern. Changes in flow rates are usually pre-planned and canoe companies are often notified so they have more information. Even if Enel (the main Italian electricity company) does need to increase flow, changes are not tsunami-like; water levels will usually increase up to about 30cm over 15 minutes. The main advice is to avoid picnicking on river islands that could be cut off, and keep an eye on children playing close to the shore.

Access and the Law

In Italy swimming in unsupervised areas is generally allowed. Every municipality usually has its own regulation, and they change fast, so try to ask locals if unsure. Sometimes the ban is cheerfully ignored by local people. Dangerous or very polluted water may be signed with Balneazione Vietata (Swimming Prohibited) but, as in the UK, with the rise in the litigation culture, many councils have been forced to post these signs in all traditional swimming places to indemnify themselves against any risk of a claim for damages. You will also find equipped beaches where lifeguards patrol. Usually you can only swim here when they are on duty.

Access and private property Public footpaths and rights of way tend to be marked by a variety of waymarks. If you can access the bank no one is likely to stop you from swimming, apart from a grumpy angler. Most national parks (Parchi Nazionali) are predominantly open access and in other areas you will find countless unmade, off-road dust tracks that are accessible by car or bike and which branch off through fields and woodlands to remote corners. Although the land is private to either side, there is generally an informal right of way along these routes. Note that wild camping – although tempting – is illegal. If you do want to camp wild, avoid farmland, never light fires, pitch late, rise early and take absolutely everything away with you.

Wild Swimming Italy

Discover the most beautiful
rivers, lakes, waterfalls
and hot springs of Italy

Words:
Michele Tameni

Photography:
Michele Tameni

Editing:
Candida Frith-MacDonald
Jessica Farmer
Fiona Wild
Michael Lee
Daniel Start

Proofing:
Michael Lee
Alessio Troiano
Laura Tameni

Design and Layout:
Oliver Mann
Marcus Freeman

Series Concept:
Daniel Start

UK Distribution:
Central Books Ltd
99 Wallis Road, London, E9 5LN
Tel +44 (0)845 458 9911
orders@centralbooks.com

Published by:
Wild Things Publishing Ltd.
Freshford, Bath, BA2 7WG
BA2 7WG, United Kingdom
hello@wildthingspublishing.com

hello@wildthingspublishing.com
hello@wildswimming.com

Author acknowledgements: Thanks to Laura Malzanini who travelled with me in this incredible journey, and for her support, help and love. Thanks also to every one who shared with me the experience of being wild in some awesome places, Alessio Troiano, Laura Tameni, Luca Domeneghini, Sebastiano Stefana, Andrea Ghidini, Frabrizio Tameni, Elia e Milena Adessa and their wonderful children. Thanks to my Mother, for her support and help, and for raising me with a wild spirit. Thanks to Wilma Adessa for her help in the translation, and again Laura Tameni, Alessio Troiano and Stefano Bennati for their important reviews of the text. Thanks to Daniel Start for his support, inspiration and for believing in me and in this project. Finally thanks to all the wild swimmer we met who shared their knowledge in exchange of a smile.

Further reading:

Orobie : i sentieri dell'acqua : 34 facili escursioni alla scoperta di sorgenti, cascate e corsi d'acqua di Lucio Benedetti, Chiara Carissoni (2011 Edizioni Junior)

Le spiagge dell'Appennino ligure. Alla scoperta di oasi incantevoli nell'entroterra, di Picco Michele (2006 Le Mani-Microart'S).

Canyoning nel Nord Italia di Pascal van Duin (2009 TopCanyon)